The Evolutionary Mindset
Stop Changing, Start Evolving

by Amy Washburn

Copyright © 2025 Amy Washburn

All rights reserved. No part of this publication may be reproduced in part or in whole or transmitted in any form or by any means, electronic or mechanical, including photocopying, recording, or via any information storage retrieval system now known or to be invented, without permission in writing from the author, except by a reviewer who wishes to quote brief passages in connection with a review written for inclusion in a print or online magazine, newspaper or broadcast.

For press inquiries, contact the author at Info@TheEvolutionaryMindset.com

First Edition March 2025

Published by Washburn Leadership Press

Boise, Idaho

ISBN:979-8-9933747-1-7

Editor: Kelly Lydick at The Story Laboratory

www.writeeditdesignlab.com

Table of Contents

Dedication 8
The Evolutionary Mindset: Introduction 11
Chapter 1 17
    The Case for Evolution 17
    Why the Word "Change" No Longer Works 23
    Change vs. Evolution: What's the Difference? 24
    Why This Matters Now 26
Chapter 2 32
    How Our Brains Work: Understanding Our Wiring 32
    Avoid Pain. Find Joy. Run Efficiently. 36
    Bias, Blind Spots & Brain Shortcuts 41
    Rewiring Is Possible 47
    Spot the Trigger. Rewrite the Story. 51
Chapter 3 55
    The Behavior Compass: Mapping What Drives Us 55
    Behavior Mapping – Connecting the Dots 73
Chapter 4 82
    Calibrate the Compass – How Evolution Ready Are You? 82
    Try This: A Sample Mindset Scan 86
Chapter 5 92
    Emotional Stamina: The Inner Evolution Engine 92
Chapter 6 105
    Discomfort: Fear-Based Resistance vs. Emotion-Driven
    Momentum 105
    Common Signs of Fear-Based Resistance 118
Chapter 7 121
    Triggers: Understanding the Story You Tell Yourself 121
    Status Quo Bias: "It's Fine. Everything Is Fine." 123
    Loss Aversion: "What Might I Lose If This Goes Wrong?" ... 126
    Confirmation Bias: "I Knew It. This Always Happens." 128
Chapter 8 154
    Reaction vs. Response 154

The Intention Gap 156
Chapter 9 170
Consistency, Not Intensity 170
Chapter 10 176
Presence Over Pressure 176
Chapter 11 193
You Go First 193
References 202
Acknowledgments 205
About the Author 207
Before You Go… 208
Worksheets & Tools 211
The Behavior Compass Worksheet 212
The Behavior Mapping Worksheet 217
The Intention Gap Quick Guide 221
Trigger Reflection Worksheet 224
Compass Check-In 228

Dedication

For the ones who don't just survive change, they evolve through it.

For every leader who's been told to "stay the course" and dared to build a better one instead.

And to my family, your belief in me anchored every word of this book.

Part I
Why Mindset Matters

The Evolutionary Mindset: Introduction

Let's get real: change is exhausting.

Not just hard. Not just uncomfortable. Exhausting. And it's not because we're weak or lazy, it's because most change efforts in organizations today are either too scattered or too confusing. Period.

Here's what I've learned over the past 20+ years in HR: People don't resist change because they're stuck in their ways. They resist because no one's made it clear. And they burn out not because they're dramatic, but because no one's made the process focused.

These are the two biggest barriers to change:

- Change fatigue → happens when there's too much going on with no real direction.
- Change resistance → happens when there's too little clarity on what's going on and why.

Sound familiar?

I once had a leader call me mid-project, a huge initiative, with lots of eyes on it, and say: "I just don't get why we're doing this." That statement stopped me cold. Because if he didn't get it, you better believe his team didn't either. I started poking around, asking questions, and it didn't take long to realize what was happening: fear, resistance, burnout, and a deep, collective wish for just one quarter where something wasn't changing. They were stuck in a change they didn't ask for and didn't want. But let's be honest, that world doesn't exist anymore.

We live in a time where change isn't just constant, it's relentless. And most organizations are trying to lead through it with frameworks that feel more like spreadsheets than survival guides. It's no wonder people feel like they're playing a game where the rules shift mid-play, and somehow, they're still expected to win.

So, what do we do?

We stop "changing" and start *evolving*.

Over the years, I've come to see that change isn't something we survive, it's something we grow through. And the difference between just getting through change and evolving through it? Mindset. This isn't about motivational fluff. This is about practical, powerful, Monday-morning tools you can actually use.

Some people fight change tooth and nail. Others quietly ghost it, nodding along in meetings and then doing the same thing they've always done. And a few, just a few, lean in with curiosity. They ask questions. They look for opportunities. They take the uncertainty and use it to grow.

These are not people with more energy or optimism. They are not change junkies or superstars. They just saw change not as an interruption, but as an evolution. And that mindset shift changes everything.

I didn't always think this way. Early in my career, change felt like something to survive, not something to step into. I was the person who quietly thought, *Here we go again,* every time a new program or initiative rolled out. My focus wasn't on possibility; it was on getting through it with as little disruption as possible. Looking back, I can see how much energy I wasted bracing for impact instead of building capacity to adapt. I had created a whole routine around holding my breath until the storm passed.

Thankfully, I had mentors who disrupted that routine and showed me a different way. One of the first was my high school drill team coach, Christy Deshazo. She had a sixth sense for what wasn't working and absolutely no hesitation about changing direction, even mid-routine. One second, we'd be running the choreography, and the next she'd stop the music, clap her hands, and call out, "Nope. That's not working. Let's change it." And during my senior year, I found myself navigating a very difficult situation. She taught me something I'll never forget: you don't need a title to lead, you just need courage to step in, name what's real, and help yourself and others move forward.

At the time, I didn't know that these situations would become two of the most important leadership lessons of my life. Change isn't scary if you trust your ability to evolve with it. When people believe in their own ability to grow, stretch, and adapt, they stop seeing change as something that happens to them. They start seeing it as something they can shape. That belief is powerful, and it's something you can build.

Later in my career, I had a leader and mentor, Leon Barnes, who gave me another piece of wisdom I still carry today: "If everything is important, then nothing is." It was his way of reminding me that leadership isn't about trying to boil the ocean. It's not about chasing every shiny object or stretching people so thin that nothing gets the attention it deserves. Focus is what creates movement. Two or three priorities, done with clarity and consistency, will outpace a dozen scattered efforts every time.

That lesson is at the heart of this book. An evolutionary mindset doesn't mean doing more; it means doing what matters, with intention. When change feels relentless, the leaders who thrive aren't the ones running faster in every direction. They're the ones steady enough to choose what to carry forward, clear enough to let go of the rest, and brave enough to say "not now" to what doesn't align.

And then there's my family, especially my mom and dad. When I was a kid, we moved cross-country, and I didn't understand why everything had to change. Years later, I repeated that pattern with my own family, and watching my daughter struggle with those moves reminded me of something they taught me: You don't have to love change to grow from it. You just have to stay open to it.

Over time, I've realized that mindset is more than just a strategy; it's a skill. And in today's fast-moving world, it's one we all need to build. Business today demands it. The organizations that are thriving are the ones leveraging an Evolutionary Mindset. They're growing through change, not just surviving it.

Those experiences shaped the mindset that's guided my entire career. It's why I can walk into a room of skeptical leaders and get them to see what's really going on beneath the surface. It's why I can help teams that are stuck, burned out, or just plain tired of "another new thing." Because I've been there. I know what it feels like to be on both sides of the equation.

This book is a guide for you, your team, and your entire organization. It's for the HR leaders, the culture builders, the executives, and even the team leaders who are just trying to keep people sane in the midst of chaos.

Inside, you'll find stories, science, exercises, and real-talk reflections. No fluff. No filler. Just practical ways to shift how you think about change, and how you help others do the same.

If you're looking for a quick weekend read that will actually make your Monday better? You're in the right place.

So, grab your coffee, get comfy, and let's rewire the way you think about change.

Starting now.

Chapter 1

The Case for Evolution

Meet Jen.

It's 1:45 p.m., and on her desk is the leftover Starbucks cup from this morning with the half-eaten bacon, Gouda sandwich she shouldn't have eaten. She instantly regretted the decision and knew she should have gotten the healthier egg bites, but they just don't taste as good. I'll try to eat cleaner tomorrow. Again. She thought. On the wall of her cube is the photo holiday card she had made this year for friends and family. She found the unopened card handing off the corner of Ben's desk, who sits 3 cubes in front of her. After the holiday season, Ben transferred to another department and left it there after packing up his desk, so she took it back. She never really liked him much anyway. The photo hangs above a plant that she has named Gloria; it seems to be the only thing thriving under the fluorescent lights.

She scans her emails and sees the typical variety of items. There are emails marked urgent, flagged emails from two days ago she still hasn't been able to get to, and 91 unread emails from last week. As she is scanning her calendar to see what meetings she can decline so she can get caught up, on her screen, a calendar invite appears that is titled *Business Update*. She quickly scans to see who was invited, and it is everyone in her department, as well as another department. She braces for impact and immediately starts to think, "Here we go again. I guess it's our turn now." There has been a slew of layoffs and restructurings in the past 6 months, and she has been worried that she will be next.

The last time she saw an email like this half of the department was shuffled. She lost teammates she depended on and ended up next to Carl, who had unique culinary habits that typically involved tuna sandwiches and reheated salmon. He was also a speakerphone evangelist. "Can you hear me now, Steph?" he'd bellow, as if volume could replace reception.

Her calendar gets hit again, and her 1:1 with her boss gets cancelled for tomorrow. "Shit." She whispers under her breath. Her pulse quickens. The timing is brutal. She just forked out $2,500.00 to keep her car from dying, $500 at the vet after her Lab, Moose, swallowed an entire leather glove he found at the park, and soccer dues for her son are looming. Layoffs aren't just a work problem; they're a life problem. And Jen can't afford one more surprise right now.

At 1:58, she opens the "Business Update" email and reads the single sentence that says nothing and everything: "Please join at 2:00 p.m. for important organizational updates." She swallows. She can feel her throat is dry. She checks the mirror tile on her monitor, hair decent, hope invisible. She clicks "Join."

The first minute is a bingo card of corporate ambiance. Someone's mic is hot, paper shuffling, a distant microwave beep, the unmistakable sound of a toddler negotiating for snacks, someone's dog is barking at the Amazon delivery, again. "You're on mute," three people say in chorus to a fourth who is not, in fact, speaking. Cameras flicker on and off like lightning bugs.

Finally, leadership tiles appear popping up like the Brady Bunch. Bright smiles, eyes looking around. Carefully staged bookshelves in the background. Jen exhales. Smiles usually mean safety. Maybe no one's losing their job. The smile, however, has a twin: the one she's seen before that precedes the phrase "We're excited to announce…" in the same tone most people reserve for "There's been an incident."

Then, she hears the words: merge, integration, synergy, and her brain, ever a team player, politely excuses itself to stare out the window. It returns in time to catch the part about technology. "We'll be adopting the other team's platform," the VP says, "It's not quite ready for how we use it yet, but we're getting there."

Jen's mouth makes a small, involuntary smile that is not a smile. She pictures "not quite ready," and she knows what that means. "We're getting there" is the corporate equivalent of "the check is in the mail" and "I'll circle back," a phrase that has escorted many a half-baked tool into full-blown production. It's a future of endless workarounds, late nights, and the slow bleed of her patience and everyone else's, trying to do the best with what they have.

The chat pings alive.

"Will there be training?"

"What's the go-live?"

"Does it integrate with our reporting?"

"I think my screen froze."

"Same."

The VP answers three of them and promises to "follow up" on the rest. Anthony jumps in, earnest enough to adapt. "Team, we've got this." He means it. Jen believes he believes it. Belief, she's learned, is necessary, but insufficient. You also need the part where systems work, and people trust them enough to use them without swearing softly at their monitors. Her colleague Priya DMs: "Do we know if the dashboard customizations carry over?" Jen replies: "Define 'know.'" Priya sends the single tear laughing emoji, the one that says, "ha-ha but also help."

And there it is. Jen realizes she's not bracing because she hates change. She likes growth. She's allergic to chaos and the lack of clarity. What's punishing isn't the newness; it's the vagueness, the way change keeps arriving each quarter with failing instructions: "Solve for x. Also, what is math?"

The VP moves to Q&A; the smiles soften. "We're confident this is the right direction," he says. Jen doesn't doubt the direction. She doubts the path. She knows how this story goes when it's just "change." People white-knuckle it. They copy-paste workarounds from a doc that someone built at 2 a.m. They become less honest in meetings because honesty sounds like "I can't keep this pace," and who wants to audition for "most replaceable" in a reorg?

Jen exhales, long and quiet. The call is still going, the plan is still fuzzy, the tech is still "getting there." She can't control any of that. What she can control is whether she treats this like a fire drill or a renovation. Fire drills are frantic; you sprint, panic, and forget your keys. Renovations are messy, but intentionally you clear space, cover what matters, and expect dust before progress.

When the VP thanks everyone for their "partnership," the tiles start disappearing. A ping pops up from Priya: "We good?" Jen types back: "We'll be good if we treat this like evolution, not a sprint. Call me after?" She adds a calm-sea gif, half reassurance, half wishful thinking, given the actual forecast looks more like sideways rain.

She ends the call and presses the heel of her hand against her chest. She whispers the anchor she's been practicing since the last upheaval: *Respond, don't react. Discomfort isn't danger.* Around her, chairs scrape back as colleagues log off, a printer whirs to life, and someone sighs the universal sigh of *"here we go again."*

As the meeting wrapped up, a message popped up on Jen's screen. It was a DM from Elena: "I'm not sure what to say in these meetings. I guess I'll just wait and see how things shake out." Jen paused before replying, "I get it. I'm choosing to focus on what I can do next, and focus on what is in my control. Want to connect tomorrow and grab a coffee so we can chat?" Elena answered with a simple thumbs-up emoji. It was subtle, but Jen knew that for Elena, silence wasn't agreement. It was her way of bracing until the ground felt steady enough to step forward.

Jen straightens in her seat, steadier now. Not because the news was good, but because she remembered where her footing is. Change can be dropped into your inbox. Evolution starts in the chair you're sitting in.

Jen's steadiness in that moment doesn't erase the reality: no one leaves a meeting like that excited. Because this is what change so often feels like: destabilizing, unclear, relentless. It rattles you, not because you're weak or dramatic, but because your brain is wired to treat it that way.

That thud in your chest, the sweaty palms, the tunnel vision? That's not overreaction, it's biology. It's the same primal alarm system our ancestors relied on when they came face-to-face with a saber-toothed tiger. Different predator, same nervous system.

Why? Because when faced with unexpected change, your brain's alarm system takes over, preparing you to fight, flight, or freeze. And while our ancestors were escaping literal predators, your brain doesn't distinguish the difference between being chased through the jungle and a surprise organizational change. Said plainly, your brain doesn't distinguish the difference between an existential threat and a situational change, a concept echoed by cognitive neuroscience research at Harvard (Barrett, 2021, HBR). Your brain sees both as a threat for survival. Why does this happen? Most people think you only have one amygdala, but you actually have two (experts just use the singular form of the word). Take your fingertips and press them gently on your temple, just above where your jawbone connects to your skull, and imagine pointing inward, toward the center of your brain. You have located your amygdala. Your amygdala plays a critical role in processing your emotions and forming memories. This is why when you hear a particular sound or smell something, it can trigger a very powerful memory. (Fitzduff, 2021).

Why the Word "Change" No Longer Works

For decades, the word *change* has been the centerpiece of corporate strategy decks, transformation projects, and endless PowerPoint presentations. We've seen it plastered on banners, baked into quarterly plans, and used as the rally cry for yet another organizational "refresh." But the way we've defined and approached change? It's no longer working. It's reactive. Episodic. Imposed. It arrives like an uninvited guest and demands that everyone make room. You know the one. The one that keeps changing the thermostat in the middle of the night so that everyone sweats to death and then denies it in the morning. Yeah, *that one*.

Most organizations treat change like a crisis to manage rather than a skill to master. And most people treat it like something to survive rather than something to grow through. We throw around phrases like "resistance to change" and "change champions," but we rarely stop to ask:

What mindset are we expecting people to adopt, and have we equipped them for it?

But what if change wasn't something we endured? What if it became something we evolved through, intentionally, steadily, and with purpose? What if our goal wasn't just to roll out the change, but to grow our capacity to navigate whatever comes next?

This is where the concept of the Evolutionary Mindset begins. It's the shift from change as an interruption to *evolution as a rhythm*. A natural, ongoing process, not a jolt to the system, but a forward motion embedded in how we think, how we lead, and how we build cultures that adapt instead of break.

Change vs. Evolution: What's the Difference?

If we're going to build a culture that truly adapts, we need to get clear on the language we use. *Change* and *evolution* are not the same thing. They may sound similar in strategy decks, but they feel radically different in practice, and they lead to very different outcomes. That's where the difference between change and evolution occurs. One keeps you afloat. The other moves you forward.

Let's break it down:

Change	Evolution
• Episodic • Often Imposed • Centered on fixing problems • Short-term & reactive • Solved immediate pain points • Driven by urgency • Typically top-down • Ends when the project ends	• Ongoing • Chosen & owned • Focused on growth & progress • Long-term & proactive • Builds sustainable strength • Driven by purpose • Often co-created & team-led • Becomes part of how the organization operates

A team experiencing change might get a new org chart, a shiny new system, or a surprise announcement in their inbox. But a team that's evolving is rethinking how they work together altogether. Change tweaks the system. Evolution transforms it.

This mindset shift toward evolution is subtle, but it changes everything. It's the difference between surviving the quarter and shaping the next decade.

Organizations that evolve don't just respond to disruption; they anticipate it. They build cultures that grow through uncertainty. They're not clinging to what used to work; they're building what works next. They aren't just talking about the current project they are working on, they are starting to brainstorm on the next one around the corner. They create intentional time and space to include the Evolutionary Mindset framework in their day-to-day activities. It becomes part of their vernacular and their intentional habits. Organizations that evolve don't respond to disruption; they anticipate it. According to Korn Ferry (2023), when organizations evolve well, they consistently outperform peers in adaptability and employee engagement as well.

So, ask yourself: Are you changing because you *have to*, or evolving because you *choose to*? The answer could define your trajectory.

In a world moving faster than ever, change is the baseline. Evolution is the advantage.

Why This Matters Now

Understanding the neuroscience of resistance is just the first step. Change, by its nature, is uncomfortable. But when we reframe it, not as something to fear but as an opportunity to evolve, we open the door to growth.

In researching this book and speaking with hundreds of leaders from HR executives to CEO's, one theme kept surfacing. When I asked them, "What is it that is impacting their organization the most?" They all said the same thing: "Change fatigue and finding a way to shift employee mindsets faster." This shouldn't be surprising to you. It wasn't to me. Change has always been constant in organizations, but the pandemic of 2020 set change into motion at a rapid pace that hasn't slowed down but rather has accelerated the pace at which we change. It also normalized constant instability in where and how you work and how business is conducted. It rushed in new technologies and innovations and propelled the markets forward with demands needing to be met as they had never been before. The need hasn't stopped or slowed down. The pandemic has made the pace acceptable and the demand mandatory. It's not a question of whether we can change as people and organizations. It's a demand to change before the need is recognized. It's a "get ahead now" or "get left behind" market. Change has always been constant in organizations, but McKinsey's 2023 State of Organizations report found a sharp increase in post-pandemic stress: Only half of leaders feel their organizations are equipped for future shocks, and employee exhaustion and complexity-related fatigue have surged, up by more than 40% since 2022 (McKinsey, 2023).

The challenge with the need is that while the tangible weight of this need can almost be felt by our workforce, how our brains are wired has not changed. It has created a clear division between those who have an Evolutionary Mindset and those who do not. Let's be clear for a moment. No one was born with an Evolutionary Mindset. It is learned. It is only learned through intentional practice and application by individuals, teams, and organizations. Because rewiring how the brain sees change takes time and practice, leaders are now under pressure to upskill their workforce, not eventually, but now. This isn't a nice-to-have skill set. It isn't a skill that only the most successful people exhibit anymore. It is a necessary practice if an organization wants to be competitive and thrive. How our brains are wired has not changed. And that explains much of the friction gap of today's resistance to workplace transformation.

We saw this earlier with Jen. It wasn't the announcement itself that shook her; it was the vagueness, the whiplash, the sense that her footing could be pulled out with every new "business update." Her reaction wasn't laziness or resistance. It was biology colliding with the pace of organizational demands. Multiply Jen's moment across a workforce, and you start to understand why change fatigue feels less like an individual weakness and more like a collective nervous system under siege.

There is a human element to this as well. I was recently at lunch with a friend who has traditionally loved her job and where she worked. She found it interesting, challenging, and collaborative. Her needs were always being met by her employer. The way she spoke about her job made me want to work where she was employed. Then, at lunch, I asked the simple question, "How's work going?" She responded, "It's brutal right now. We have made three significant changes in the past 12 months, and the last one we made was because the first one didn't go well. They had to backtrack. The teams can't process the amount of change that is coming at them, and the leadership team isn't really doing the best job communicating and connecting the dots. We are all spinning right now."

This is a classic example of the human reaction to change fatigue. As we sat and talked about what we were seeing in different markets, the one consistent thread was this one: People are tired. Our brains can't process all the change fast enough in the world, at work, or in their homes. They are all interconnected. And, if you are part of a company that hasn't invested in an Evolutionary Mindset practice, you might be reliant upon yourself to learn it on your own.

I truly believe we all get a choice every day of where we work and how we live. And those choices all start with what we think, then how we think about the world, and what is happening around us. If you know you struggle with change, you are not alone. It is normal to struggle with change. It's normal to fight against what is uncomfortable. It is normal to question, "Why?" But, if you knew that the Evolutionary Mindset could help you reduce stress, make you better equipped to handle change, and come home happier every day, wouldn't that be worth the effort? No one will ever care more about your development than you. (Well, except maybe your mother.) By reading this book and sharing the content with those who work and live with you, you have a chance to not only change your life but also change the lives around you.

And here's the good news: Evolution doesn't demand perfection. It demands progress. And when leaders equip their teams with the tools and mindset found in this book, they create the conditions for something far more valuable than just surviving the next shift; they build the muscle for sustainable momentum.

In the next chapter, we'll explore how our brains are wired, so you can better understand *why* change feels like such a struggle. It's not about survival. It's about creating something better. Because when we stop resisting change and start evolving through it, we move closer to the future we've always wanted, and we begin to build a culture that doesn't just survive change but *thrives* because of it.

Chapter 2

How Our Brains Work: Understanding Our Wiring

Let's get something straight: your brain may be the most powerful organ in your body, but it also acts like a toddler with a crayon: stubborn, impulsive, and absolutely convinced it knows what's best.

It doesn't like surprises. It doesn't like discomfort. And it really doesn't like being told what to do.

That's not a character flaw. It's wiring.

Your brain's #1 job is to keep you alive. Not to help you innovate. Not to make sure your team hits its Q3 numbers. And certainly not to cheer you on through your organization's latest restructuring. It's just trying to get you through the day with the least amount of risk possible, preferably while wearing sweatpants and doing things it already knows how to do.

And when something new *does* show up? Like a new leader, a new system, or yet another "strategic shift" from the C-suite? That inner toddler starts to panic. "This doesn't feel safe. I don't like this. Let's go back to what we were doing before. Where's my snack?"

Now here's the kicker: this isn't just a funny metaphor. It's actually how your brain operates when it detects uncertainty.

It throws up resistance not because it's trying to sabotage you, but because it's trying to protect you. As Fitzduff (2021) explains in her neuroscience research, the amygdala's overreaction is an evolved defense system, not a flaw. Understanding this wiring helps leaders lead with empathy rather than urgency. From pain. From failure. From the unknown.

Take Jen's team. When the latest "strategic shift" email landed, she pressed her palm to her chest and whispered, "Respond, don't react. Discomfort isn't danger." Priya sighed and muttered something about "six more months of late nights and extra logins." Anthony didn't say much at all; he just opened LinkedIn in another tab and started scrolling. Same email, three different responses. None of them are irrational. All of them were weird.

Which is why even the *best* change efforts stall when leaders forget one very important truth: You can't outsmart your brain's wiring. But you *can* retrain it.

And that's what this chapter is about.

Your Brain Isn't Being Difficult. It's Just Doing Its Job.
Here's the thing most leaders forget (or were never taught): when someone resists change, it's not because they're negative, lazy, or stuck in their ways. It's because their brain is doing exactly what it was designed to do, protect them from danger. That "danger" may not be a bear in the woods, but to

the brain, a new org structure or unfamiliar expectation can feel just as threatening.

This is the fight, flight, or freeze response in action. It's ancient wiring. The moment uncertainty shows up, the amygdala, the brain's alarm system, takes over. Logic takes a back seat. Emotion slams the gas pedal. And suddenly, even your top performers can seem unrecognizable: one lashes out in meetings (fight), another avoids their inbox (flight), and a third seems checked out altogether (freeze). None of this is personal. It's neurological.

Remember Anthony? He's the steady voice in the room, "We've got this team", the kind of comment that sounds confident enough to settle the group. But if you watch closely, you'll see the calculation behind it. He wants to believe what he's saying, but the constant churn wears him down. He's not storming out of meetings or freezing in silence; he's the tenured high performer who projects optimism while quietly wondering how many more rounds of 'new and improved' he can take. If the right role with a bigger title and paycheck came along, he'd consider it in a heartbeat. On the surface: engagement. Underneath: fatigue, mixed with ambition. That tension is its own kind of flight response, the kind that happens not in the meeting, but in a future exit interview.

And Priya? Classic fighter, but not in a reckless way. She's sharp, outspoken, and usually the first to spot gaps others gloss over. If there's a new system rolling out, she'll be the one at the table saying, "Why are we fixing something that wasn't broken?" Her pushback is protective. She fights because she cares about efficiency and fairness, even if it sometimes comes off as combative.

Then there's Elena, the freeze response in action. Dependable and steady, but when change hits, her instinct is to pull back. She nods in meetings, takes careful notes, but rarely speaks up until someone else voices what she's been thinking. For Elena, change feels less like a challenge to engage and more like something to endure.

And Jen? She used to hold her breath through moments like these, waiting for the wave to pass. But she's been practicing something different, the Evolutionary Mindset. Instead of freezing, she pauses. She whispers her anchor phrase, "Respond, don't react. Discomfort isn't danger," and chooses her next step with intention. She isn't fearless, but she is learning to steady herself in the middle of uncertainty. That shift makes her more than just another person enduring change. It makes her a guide for the team.

Understanding this doesn't excuse unproductive behavior, but it explains it, and that matters. Because when we understand the root of resistance, we stop labeling people as "difficult" and start leading them with empathy. Resistance isn't a character flaw. It's a natural signal that someone's internal safety system has been tripped.

This physiological reaction, known as the defense cascade, is triggered by the amygdala responding to perceived threat or uncertainty, initiating fight, flight, or freeze behaviors that override higher-level reasoning (Rabinoff, M. 2015).

And this is where the *evolutionary mindset* begins to shift the game. Evolution doesn't happen in survival mode; it happens in clarity, safety, and intention. When you help people feel seen, understood, and equipped, not forced, you create the psychological space for change to become growth. And that's when real momentum starts to build.

Avoid Pain. Find Joy. Run Efficiently.

If you've ever wondered why your team resists a new idea, even one that's clearly better, faster, and smarter, the answer probably isn't about logic. It's about wiring.

Beneath the surface of every decision we make are three primary motivators that drive human behavior. These aren't corporate buzzwords or self-help fluff. These are survival instincts, hard-coded into the brain like default settings:

1. **Avoid Pain**
2. **Find Joy**
3. **Run Efficiently**

These three drivers shape how people react to change, how they engage with work, and how quickly (or slowly) they adapt. Let's break them down:

1. Avoid Pain: "Don't make this harder than it has to be."

The brain's first job is to protect you from harm, physical, emotional, and psychological. It doesn't distinguish between danger and discomfort. So, when people push back on change, it's often not because they're unwilling, but because their brain perceives pain ahead. Extra work. Fear of failure. Judgment. Loss of status or identity. It's safer to dig in or check out than to risk falling short.

Think about the last time a new system rolled out. Did your team say, "Great! Something we've never done before that will require lots of learning and late nights!" No? Exactly.

2. Find Joy: "Give me something that feels good, or at least familiar."

We're wired to seek out reward, big or small. That dopamine hit from checking off a to-do list? That comfort in knowing exactly where to click in the old software? That's joy. And the kicker is, familiarity often *feels* like joy to the brain, even when the old way isn't ideal.

This is why people often stick with outdated processes, even if they're inefficient. The old way might be clunky, but at least they *know* it. It doesn't require risk or extra brainpower.

3. Run Efficiently: "What's the easiest path forward?"

The brain is a high-efficiency machine. Once it learns a routine, whether it's a morning commute or how to prep for a meeting, it locks it in. Think of it like autopilot. And when change comes in and rewrites the steps? The brain throws a little tantrum. It has to work harder now. It doesn't like that. Efficiency isn't about laziness. It's about survival. The brain wants to conserve energy for big threats (see: toddler with a crayon and a lot of opinions). Recall in Chapter 1, the 2023 McKinsey State of Organizations report, which showed that change fatigue had increased by more than 40% (McKinsey, 2023). That's why change, even good change, feels exhausting. It disrupts our neurological shortcuts.

When you understand these drivers, you stop asking, *"Why are people so resistant?"* and start asking, *"Which of these drivers feels threatened right now?"*

This is where the *evolutionary mindset* starts to come alive. Leaders who evolve don't just push harder; they get curious. They learn to see beneath the resistance and speak to what's actually going on. And when you design change with these three drivers in mind, minimizing pain, creating moments of joy, and showing people how it can eventually become more efficient? You don't just roll out a plan. You get buy-in.

The Habit Highway

The brain is a master of efficiency. Every time you think a thought, speak a phrase, or react a certain way, it carves a tiny groove in your neural network. Do it once, and it's a faint trail. Do it a few dozen times, and you've got a dirt path. Do it for years, consciously or not, and that trail turns into a six-lane interstate, complete with mile markers, an exit ramp, and a Starbucks off to the side. It's not just a habit. It's a neural highway.

This is what neuroscientists mean when they say, *"What fires together, wires together."* The more often two neurons are activated at the same time, the stronger the connection becomes. Your brain essentially says, "Ah, this again? Great, I know this route," and takes it without thinking. It doesn't care if the route leads somewhere productive or not. Its priority is speed, not strategy.

This is known in neuroscience as the Hebbian learning, a fundamental principle of synaptic plasticity introduced by Donald O. Hebb, in which repeated, simultaneous neuron activation strengthens their connection, making that pathway automatic and fast, even if it's unproductive (Hebbian theory, Hebb, 1949).

Now, here's where this matters for leaders: our teams, and let's be honest, ourselves too, have built up mental highways for how we respond to change. For some, it's an immediate no. For others, it's cautious compliance while secretly hoping it all blows over. These responses aren't personality quirks. They're pathways. And they've been reinforced over time by past experiences, company culture, and whether previous "big changes" ended in burnout or broken trust.

Eventually, the brain begins to equate *change* with *danger*, not because every change *is* dangerous, but because the wiring was built that way through repetition. Each frustrating rollout, each poorly explained pivot, each time someone wasn't consulted but was expected to comply, it all reinforced the same pattern: "Change means chaos. Prepare to protect yourself." *The Harvard Business Review* notes that repeated psychological threats during change reduces trust and engagement, especially when employees feel they have no influence (HBR 2023).

This is why even the most forward-thinking leaders can feel stuck. Why high-potential employees freeze in the face of a new strategy. It's not a lack of ability; it's the muscle memory of the mind pulling them back to what feels safe.

But here's the good news: the brain isn't fixed. It's malleable. Which means it can be rewired. You can build new highways, but you have to walk the new path over and over again before it feels natural. This takes practice, not perfection. It takes intention, not just enthusiasm. And it takes environments where people are allowed to experiment, mess up, and try again without fear of being labeled resistant, negative, or "not a team player."

This is where the *evolutionary mindset* starts to shine. It acknowledges the reality of the wiring, and gives people a new framework to reroute it. Not with forced optimism or vague encouragement, but with clarity, consistency, and small repeated actions that tell the brain, "Hey, we're safe. You don't have to fight this." Over time, those new thoughts, responses, and conversations carve fresh grooves. And eventually? You've built a better road.

Bias, Blind Spots & Brain Shortcuts

Let's be real, your brain is always looking for a shortcut. Not because it's lazy, but because it's trying to keep up. Every second of every day, your mind is processing millions of bits of information: conversations, notifications, facial expressions, calendar reminders, that slightly weird tone in your boss's email... It never stops. So, your brain, being the efficient little processor that it is, starts making assumptions. Fast ones. Automatic ones. Ones it doesn't even tell you it's making.

These mental shortcuts are called cognitive biases, and they're not reserved for "other people." We all have them. Daniel Kahneman's foundational research on heuristics confirms that cognitive shortcuts shape nearly every decision, especially under pressure (Kahneman & Tversky, 1974). They're the background noise of our decision-making, constantly whispering, *"Just go with what you know."*

But even when change doesn't feel overtly threatening, there's another layer working against us, one that's harder to spot because it's baked into how we think. Our brains are constantly taking shortcuts to keep up, and while that's great for survival, it's not always great for decision-making. This is where biases come in, not as character flaws, but as default settings that can quietly steer us off course without us even realizing it.

Status Quo Bias

There's a reason people cling to what's familiar, even if it's outdated, inefficient, or actively driving them crazy. It's called status quo bias: the tendency to prefer things to remain as they are, simply because they're known. It's not that people believe the current process is the best one; it's that the idea of switching to something unknown feels too mentally and emotionally taxing. In the context of change, this shows up as that inner shrug: "It's not great, but at least it's familiar." And familiar, to the brain, often feels like safe. Studies have shown that employees often resist change not due to logic, but due to a perceived loss of stability, even when the new option is clearly better (Samuelson & Zeckhauser, 1988; Jost et al., 2004). Status quo bias is one of the biggest hidden obstacles to transformation, because it doesn't yell. It just gently lulls people back into inertia.

For Priya, this bias shows up as fierce protection of what works. She's quick to challenge a new system with, "Why are we fixing something that wasn't broken?" But underneath the sharp tone is something quieter: concern for the people around her. She knows how stretched her team already feels, and the thought of yet another "upgrade" lands like a threat to their bandwidth, not a gift. Her resistance isn't defiance; it's her brain clinging to the stability of the familiar and shielding the team from more disruption than they can handle.

When she pushes back, it's not because she can't imagine a better way. It's because the old way, clunky as it might be, has at least proven it won't collapse under pressure. To Priya, change equals risk, and unless the payoff is crystal clear, she will plant her flag in the ground and fight to protect what's already working. That stance can frustrate leaders who only see the friction, but it's also why her team trusts her, because they know she'll go to the mat for them when things feel unstable.

Loss Aversion

Then there's loss aversion, the emotional seesaw where the pain of losing something is felt more intensely than the pleasure of gaining something new. Even when people dislike their current systems, roles, or routines, they'll often hold on tightly because the idea of giving them up feels threatening. They fear losing control, competence, or identity. The irony? Many of these things were already causing frustration, but they were at least known frustrations. Nobel laureates Kahneman and Tversky found that people will go to great lengths to avoid loss, even if it means bypassing potential gains (Kahneman & Tversky, 1979). In workplaces, this is the cognitive trap that keeps people stuck in patterns they've long outgrown, simply because letting go feels riskier than staying stuck.

For Elena, loss aversion shows up in quiet ways. She rarely says no outright, but her silence speaks volumes. In meetings, she nods, jots careful notes, and waits for someone else to break the ice before she shares her thoughts. To the outside eye, it looks like compliance, even support. But inside, she's doing the math, what could she lose if she's wrong? Credibility? Time? The reputation of being steady and dependable? For Elena, the pain of risking those losses outweighs the potential gain of speaking up too soon. Her instinct is to hold back until the ground feels steady, even if it means valuable ideas go unheard in the moment.

This isn't because she lacks courage. It's because her brain equates stepping forward with danger and waiting with safety. Leaders often misinterpret this as disengagement, but in truth, it's her wiring choosing certainty over possibility. Elena's still in the game; she's just standing on the sidelines until she knows which direction the play is headed.

And here's where it gets even trickier: the brain doesn't just react to fear, it *justifies* it. It starts gathering "evidence" to support the story it's already decided is true. This is where biases start to creep in, not because someone is being difficult, but because their brain is working overtime to protect them from imagined threats. These mental shortcuts are fast, familiar, and wildly convincing. But if we don't know they're there, they'll quietly shape decisions, derail change efforts, and reinforce resistance in ways that feel logical, even when they're not.

Let's talk about fear for a minute, not the dramatic, movie-trailer kind, but the everyday, quietly sabotaging kind that shows up in work emails, new initiatives, and team dynamics. Most of the time, the fear we experience during change isn't based on something real. It's based on something *anticipated*. It's not the current situation that's overwhelming; it's all the imagined ways it could go sideways.

There's a reason the acronym F.E.A.R.: *False Expectations Appearing Real*, hits home for so many people (Coller, 2018). Because that's exactly how resistance often shows up.

Someone hears a vague announcement about "restructuring," and before they've even been given details, their brain fills in the blanks: *I'm losing my job. My team's being split up. I'm going to look incompetent.* None of it has happened yet. But the brain treats those imagined outcomes like facts. And it responds accordingly, with panic, avoidance, or passive-aggressive calendar declines.

For Anthony, fear doesn't show up as panic in the moment, it hides behind polished optimism. He's the first to say, "We've got this team," and he means it… at least partly. But the second the meeting ends, his brain starts running scenarios. What if the merger means his role shrinks? What if the new reporting structure sidelines his influence? What if someone else lands the promotion he's been eyeing? None of it has happened, but the imagined losses feel as real as facts. His confidence in the room masks the churn in his head, where he's already rehearsing worst-case org charts that don't have his name on top.

This is F.E.A.R. in action, False Expectations Appearing Real. To others, Anthony looks calm and engaged. Internally, he's bracing for a future that hasn't arrived, hedging against a status he might not get to keep. He isn't running for the door, but he is quietly calculating whether staying the course is worth it if the story in his head comes true. That tension leaves him half in, half out, projecting loyalty while his brain whispers exit strategies.

This fear-based thinking is not a flaw in our people; it's a feature of our biology. And when leaders recognize that fear often comes dressed up as "concern" or "low engagement," they can respond with empathy instead of frustration. Fear is rarely about the *facts*. It's about the *feelings* the brain has attached to the unknown.

This is where the evolutionary mindset offers a better path. It doesn't shame fear. It names it. It helps people untangle what's *real* from what's *perceived* and gives them the tools to shift back into intention, logic, and clarity. Because once you see that your fear is just a story, and not a prophecy, you can choose a better one.

Here's the kicker: these aren't just personal problems. These biases show up in boardrooms, project plans, and team dynamics every single day. They affect hiring decisions, communication strategies, and how open people are to feedback. Leaders, no matter how experienced, fall into these traps, too, especially when pressure is high and time is short. That's why the *Evolutionary Mindset* is more than just a reframe. It's a tool to disrupt these shortcuts. It invites leaders to pause before reacting, to question before deciding, and to recognize that sometimes the biggest obstacle isn't the change itself, it's the story the brain is telling about it.

And when we learn to spot those blind spots? That's when transformation gets real traction. Not because we forced people through a new process, but because we helped them *see differently*, and that is what rewires behavior at the root.

Rewiring Is Possible

Here's the part that doesn't get talked about enough: Your brain is built to change. It doesn't always *want* to, but it *can*. And that gap between capability and willingness? That's the space where transformation either ignites or flatlines. Neuroplasticity is the brain's ability to rewire itself through new experiences, repeated behavior, and intentional thought. In plain terms? You can teach your brain to take a different route. Even if it's been driving the same emotional and behavioral patterns for years. But, and this is key, it doesn't happen because you *know better*. It happens because you *practice differently*.

It's a lot like learning to cook a new recipe. The first time, you're glued to the instructions. You double-check the measurements. You question whether "a pinch" is actually a measurable unit. It's clunky and slow. But the more you make it, the easier it gets. You start to anticipate the steps. You adjust for taste. Eventually, you don't need the recipe at all, you just *know* how it's supposed to feel. That's what rewiring looks like. Not perfection from the start, but confidence built through consistency.

This is how people shift from avoidance to courage, from defensiveness to curiosity. And it's how teams move from reacting to change to actually building momentum with it. The key isn't intensity, it's consistency. Small, repeated steps. Conversations that feel slightly uncomfortable at first. Leaders who model vulnerability, clarity, and grounded decision-making. None of it feels dramatic in the moment, but over time, the cumulative effect is powerful.

That's why the *Evolutionary Mindset* isn't just about a new perspective; it's about daily habits that rewire our internal GPS. It doesn't demand that you be fearless, just that you become more *aware* of the choices you're making and the patterns you're reinforcing. Do you pause before responding? Do you name what's really going on? Do you ask better questions instead of jumping to conclusions?

Mirror Moment

What part of your wiring has been calling the shots lately, and are you following it because it's true, or just because it's familiar?

The people and teams who evolve aren't always the smartest or most experienced. They're the ones who show up curious, who notice when their old wiring is kicking in, and who are willing to do the slow work of laying a better track.

Change doesn't become less chaotic. But your response to it becomes more calibrated. And that's where your real power is.

Noticing Your Triggers

Let's get honest, most of us aren't resisting change because we're obstinate. We're resisting because something about it pokes at a sore spot we haven't fully dealt with or explored well enough. A fear of being irrelevant. A memory of when we got burned. A worry we'll look unprepared or incapable in front of our team. These aren't just emotions. They're *triggers*. And if we don't notice them, they end up driving behavior. For Jen, it was the email she received with the subject line "Business Update." She has lived through enough messy rollouts that those two words alone light up old memories of late nights, unclear directives, and shifting ground. The email itself isn't the problem; it's the story their brains instantly attach to it.

When change happens, the brain doesn't send you a polite calendar invite saying, *"Hey, just FYI, I'm about to overreact."* It just reacts. And unless you've practiced noticing the signs, tight chest, short temper, desire to bail on that meeting, you'll find yourself halfway through a meltdown before you even realize what set you off.

That's why self-awareness isn't a "nice-to-have" leadership trait anymore. It's a survival skill. The leaders and teams who evolve aren't the ones who power through without blinking. They're the ones who know when something's off, and stop to name it before it derails the room.

Most people can describe their frustration. Fewer can name the *trigger* behind it, and even fewer can spot the *story* they're telling themselves in response. That's where things get messy. Because when the story takes over, the behavior follows, and not always in helpful ways.

Let's break this down with a few real-world examples. These are moments that happen in workplaces every day. Your job isn't to judge the reaction, but to notice the story it might be reinforcing.

Spot the Trigger. Rewrite the Story.

Think back over the past month. Which of these moments have you experienced? Circle a few that hit close to home, or add your own. Then pause and ask:
What story did I tell myself in that moment? And was it actually true... or just familiar?

Trigger	Story I Told Myself
Received an email titled "Business Update" on a Friday afternoon	_____
My meeting was suddenly forwarded to a senior leader	_____
Someone else's idea got attention, mine didn't	_____
I received critical feedback from my manager	_____
A colleague got promoted before me	_____
I was left off a meeting invite or email thread	_____
I was interrupted mid-sentence in a meeting	_____

Trigger	Story I Told Myself
A direct report questioned my decision publicly	_____
A peer was praised for a team project I worked on	_____
A leadership decision was reversed or changed at the last minute	_____

Now take a breath and ask:
- What's *another* story I could have told myself?
- What part of that moment felt like a threat?
- What would it look like to respond with curiosity instead of protection?

This isn't about overthinking every interaction. It's about noticing your default responses. Because once you start catching the story early, you give yourself a chance to rewrite the response.

The best leaders I know aren't the ones who have it all figured out. They're the ones who've learned how to slow down just enough to say, *"Okay, that reaction wasn't helpful. Let me try again."* That's not a weakness. That's wisdom.

Because once you understand your wiring and spot your triggers, you've taken the most important step toward leading with *intention* instead of instinct. And that's the kind of leadership people will actually follow.

Chapter 3

The Behavior Compass: Mapping What Drives Us

A few years back, I found myself seated to the right of a leader I had been supporting for months. Let's call him David. David was the kind of leader who always looked composed. Even on a Friday, you would be hard-pressed to find one piece of lint on his sports coat. He was smart, polished, and deeply respected in the organization. People liked him, but they didn't always feel close to him. His leadership style was professional, sometimes so polished it felt untouchable. People liked him, but they didn't always feel like they knew him.

That morning, David and I were side by side in a glass-walled conference room overlooking the city skyline. Twelve team members sat scattered around a long glass table, their faces a mix of curiosity and quiet dread. Claudia tried to fill the silence with small talk about her weekend plans, while Tom seemed locked in an angry text battle on his phone, his thumbs moving furiously. Everyone looked like they would rather be anywhere else. On one side of the table sat Maria, a steady mid-level manager with twelve years in the company. She was well-regarded, dependable, the kind of leader people leaned on during chaos. She fiddled with her bracelet, her jaw tight, eyes fixed on the papers in front of her. Two seats over was Jamal, a rising star in operations, known for being sharp and outspoken, but he was silent now, shoulders tense, arms crossed. At the far end sat Aaron, a quick-witted project lead who never missed a chance to crack a sarcastic joke in the breakroom. He leaned back in his chair, spinning a pen between his fingers, his eyes darting toward the clock.

We were there to announce a change that would impact about half the group. New reporting lines. A shift in how support was structured. The kind of organizational shake-up that makes even the most secure employee wonder, *Am I next?*

The other half of the team? Not directly impacted. But if you've been in corporate life for more than a few minutes, you know the truth: no one walks away untouched. Tension doesn't stay neatly contained on one side of the org chart. It leaks. It spreads. And eventually, everyone feels it.

David leaned forward, clasped his hands, and delivered the message with steady clarity. His voice was calm, rehearsed, but not robotic. He explained the new reporting lines, the shifts in support structure, and the "opportunities" this change would bring. His delivery was steady, measured, and professional to the core. Then he did something most leaders don't: he paused, scanned the room, and said, "Any questions? Concerns? I want to hear from you."

And he waited.

Crickets.

Not a single hand. Not a single voice. Just the sterile silence of people pretending they were fine while their minds screamed something entirely different. Maria glanced down, avoiding eye contact. Jamal kept his arms locked tight, a physical barrier. Aaron raised his eyebrows, smirked almost imperceptibly, but said nothing.

It was the kind of silence that isn't peaceful; it's loaded. You could almost feel the collective thought running through the group: *Say nothing. Don't be the one to speak up. Just survive the meeting.*

When the meeting ended, people shuffled out like they were leaving a dentist's office, polite, quiet, slightly numb. A few nodded politely at David as they left, the kind of nod that says *I heard you* without actually meaning *I'm with you*. Others avoided eye contact altogether, staring at the floor as though it held the answers they were searching for.

On the surface, the meeting looked fine. But anyone who's ever led through change knows the truth: silence doesn't equal alignment.

David leaned back in his chair, exhaled slowly, and took a sip of his coffee. "That went better than I expected," he said, almost to himself.

I didn't agree. Something in the room had felt off, like a storm cloud passing overhead that never fully broke open. I turned toward him. "There's more going on here. They just haven't told us what that is yet."

Five minutes later, my phone buzzed. A group text lit up the screen. It was one of those old threads that had gone quiet for months but still lived in the background. I glanced down to see a single message that made my stomach drop and my eyebrows lift all at once.

"I hear there's a new shit show coming to theaters next week. Who's excited?"

The kicker? The text had come from someone still sitting in that conference room only minutes earlier. And judging by the quick stream of laughing emojis that followed, the rest of the team had already started chiming in.

I glanced at David, still sitting beside me, completely unaware, sipping his coffee like we had just wrapped up a solid town hall. I slid the phone across the table toward him, screen up.

He raised an eyebrow, read the message, and then looked at me. "Well," he said dryly, "I guess they're processing. Just not out loud."

"Exactly," I said. "They're saying what they really think, just not to you."

David chuckled. "Is that HR-speak for 'they think this is a dumpster fire'?"

I nodded. "That's the clinical term, yes."

We both laughed, but only for a second. Because behind the sarcasm, we knew exactly what that message meant: the team didn't feel safe enough to voice their concerns in the room where it mattered most.

And here's the leadership truth I'll never forget from that moment: what people say after the meeting is more honest than what they say in it.

The text thread wasn't just gossip. It was a signal. A flashing red light telling us that values, beliefs, thoughts, and emotions were activated beneath the surface. That's what the Behavior Compass helps us see. On the outside, you had a silent room. On the inside, you had people wrestling with emotions they didn't feel safe enough to name.

And here's the danger: when teams don't feel safe, silence becomes the default strategy. People nod in agreement, then vent in group texts. They say "sounds good" in meetings, then do the opposite behind the scenes. They withhold ideas not because they don't care, but because they don't believe their voice is safe.

That day with David, I was reminded of something Amy Edmondson's research has made crystal clear: psychological safety isn't about comfort. It's about courage. Trust isn't built in polished announcements. It's built in what happens after the slides click off and the room empties.

Because if you don't know what's underneath the silence, you'll never shift what's driving it.

Mirror Moment

What's one behavior you've been judging either in yourself or someone else that makes perfect sense when you trace it back to what's underneath?

You can't lead what you can't see.

That moment in the conference room didn't just show me misalignment; it showed me invisibility. Because behavior doesn't start with behavior. It starts with what's *underneath* it: values, beliefs, thoughts, and emotions.

These aren't "soft" things. They're directional. Foundational. They're what I call your Behavior Compass, and whether you realize it or not, yours is always pointing somewhere.

If your values are misaligned, your compass drifts. If your beliefs are outdated, your compass spins. If your thoughts are distorted, your compass confuses others. And if your emotions are unmanaged? Well, that's when the team group text starts popping off.

The Behavior Compass isn't just a framework; it's a lens. One that helps you understand *why* people react the way they do when change rolls in, and more importantly, what to do about it.

Let's walk through each element, *North, South, East, West*, and decode what's really going on when behavior feels off.

North: Your Values – What Anchors You

Let's start with North, the top of the compass. Your values. These are your non-negotiables. Your internal code. The convictions you carry into every meeting, every decision, every hard conversation. They're the "this matters" filter in your brain. And when they're clear and aligned, they act like an anchor. They hold you steady when the waters of change get rough.

But here's the catch: Values don't shout. They whisper. And if you're not paying attention, you'll miss them completely. You can feel when values are aligned. There's clarity. Stability. Even when things get chaotic, you know where your center is, and that gives you a quiet confidence most leaders don't even realize they're missing.

And you can *absolutely* feel when someone challenges them. Because when someone pushes on your values, whether they mean to or not, it doesn't just frustrate you. It rattles something deep. You feel it in your gut. In your jaw. In your sudden urge to either shut down or push back hard. That reaction? That's your internal compass sounding the alarm. Think back to that meeting with David. Maria wasn't just fiddling with her bracelet because she was nervous; her value of stability was being rattled. The change announcement hit right where her sense of security and loyalty lived, and even though she didn't voice it, her silence was her compass, sounding the alarm. Why? Because values aren't surface-level preferences. They're rooted in your lived experience. Your upbringing. Your beliefs about right and wrong. So, when someone questions or contradicts them, it doesn't feel like a disagreement. It feels like a personal attack, even if it's not. For me, some of my deepest values were shaped by the women who raised me. My grandmother had a favorite saying, *"Anything worth doing is worth doing right."* She didn't just say it, she lived it. Whether she was baking from scratch or writing a thank-you note in her signature cursive, she modeled the kind of excellence that wasn't loud, but was deeply felt. And that value stuck.

My mother instilled my faith. She would often say, *"Trust in His plan and His timing."* That wasn't just spiritual advice, it became a compass I returned to in the middle of uncertainty, decisions, and change. When everything felt like it was shifting, that truth helped me root myself in something steadier than my circumstances.

These weren't values I picked from a workshop. They were handed down. Lived in. Proven over time. And because they're so deeply embedded, when they're questioned, even unintentionally, it hits different.

And that's where values can show up as both strength and struggle.

When aligned, values provide clarity, consistency, and grounded leadership.

When misaligned or overplayed, they can become barriers.

Let's break that down:

- **When values are aligned:**
  You lead with stability, grounded decision-making, and a strong sense of purpose. You know what matters, and your team knows where you stand.
- **When values are misaligned or distorted:**
  You may cling too tightly to "the way it should be." You may become rigid, moralizing, or unwilling to bend, even when the situation calls for nuance. That's how leaders fall into what I call the *"moral high ground trap"*, where the value itself is good, but the way it's being enforced creates disconnection or resistance.

This doesn't mean you need to abandon your values. It means you need to stay *aware* of when they're helping you evolve, and when they might be unintentionally holding you stuck in place.

Let me say this clearly: Your values don't just influence your leadership, they define it.

So, ask yourself:

- What values are driving how I respond to change?
- Do those values support adaptability, or are they anchoring me in place?
- Am I clinging to a value because it's right, or because it's familiar?

- What emotions come up when someone challenges my values, and what might that be revealing?

Sometimes, the very values that once helped you succeed become the ones that keep you stuck.

The point isn't to discard them. It's to check whether they're helping you lead forward, or locking you in place.

Because when your values are misaligned with your behavior? Your team notices. And the compass starts spinning.

East: Your Beliefs – What You Accept as Truth

If values are your anchor, beliefs are your filter. They're the lens you use to interpret what's happening around you. But here's the catch: just because you believe something doesn't mean it's true.

Beliefs are shaped over time. From experience. From what worked once. From what didn't. From that leader you admired early in your career. From the one who burned you later. From company culture. From family dynamics. From faith. From pain. From hope.

And once they're formed? Your brain starts building a whole internal system to reinforce them. Beliefs are like sunrises; no two are the same, and they change over time because they are shaped by the environment.

Beliefs become the stories we tell ourselves about how the world works, and more importantly, how we think we work within it.

You've probably heard versions of these:

- "I'm not a strategic thinker."
- "If I speak up, it won't matter."
- "I have to fix everything or I've failed."
- "People don't change."
- "Leadership doesn't really want feedback, they just say that."

Now pause. Read that last one again.

Remember Jamal at the table, arms crossed, eyes fixed straight ahead? On the surface, it looked like defiance, but underneath it was a belief he had carried from past reorganizations: *Leadership doesn't really want feedback; they just want compliance.* That belief shaped his silence more than the change itself, and until it's surfaced, no amount of polished messaging can break through it.

Because that belief alone is one of the biggest blockers to team evolution I've seen in the last 20 years. Not because it's always wrong, but because once it's believed, it becomes self-fulfilling. If someone believes they'll be ignored, they stop contributing. If they believe they'll be punished for pushing back, they stop challenging. And if they believe the game is rigged, they stop playing.

That belief might have started as a reaction to a moment, but over time, it becomes an operating system. And here's where it gets tricky: Most people don't even realize their beliefs are outdated. They've worn them for so long they feel like truth.

And that's why beliefs can be both powerful tools and hidden traps.

Let's look at both sides:

- **When beliefs are aligned:**
   You gain clarity of direction, conviction in your choices, and a deeper sense of purpose. Aligned beliefs help you lead with intention and help others trust your consistency.

- **When beliefs are misaligned or outdated:**
   You may default to groupthink, become resistant to new ideas, or fall into identity-protecting behaviors. You might double down on a belief that once served you, but now prevents growth. That's when strong belief starts to look more like a blind spot than a strength.

This is why teams can sit through the same announcement and walk away with completely different stories. Because they're not hearing it through facts, they're hearing it through their filters.

And unless a leader is actively working to uncover and update those beliefs, personally and collectively, those filters will keep recycling the same behavior. No matter how great the strategy is.

Ask yourself:

- What beliefs am I holding about change? About leadership? About my team?

- Are those beliefs still true, or just familiar?
- Were they formed from clarity, or from a past experience I never really unpacked?
- What belief would I need to replace in order to lead forward more effectively?

Here's the thing: Challenging a belief doesn't mean abandoning it. Sometimes it just needs to evolve. Beliefs aren't etched in stone; they're written in pencil. And if you want to build an evolutionary culture, you've got to be willing to sharpen that pencil and edit.

Because leadership isn't about being right, it's about staying aligned. And when your beliefs are out of sync with your goals, your behavior will be too.

South: Your Thoughts – What You Tell Yourself

If beliefs are your filter, thoughts are the internal script that plays on repeat. And here's the kicker, most of the time, you don't even realize it's playing.

Thoughts run deep. Deeper than we realize. They're the private conversations you have with yourself before the meeting starts, after you've read the email, or when your idea gets dismissed for the third time. They're the quiet voice that says, *"You've got this"*, or the one that whispers, *"Why even bother?"*

And those thoughts? They shape everything.

You may think behavior begins with action. It doesn't. It begins with thought. Because what you think determines what you expect. What you expect determines how you show up. And how you show up determines whether people follow you or question you.

Here's the dangerous part: If your thoughts are distorted, everything downstream is distorted too.

Let's say your internal dialogue is quietly feeding you this message: *"My input doesn't matter here."* That thought might seem small. But suddenly, you're quieter in meetings. You stop challenging ideas. You hesitate to follow up on your instincts. The team notices a shift, but they don't see the root. All they see is disengagement.

Or, maybe your internal thought is, *"I'm supposed to have all the answers."* So, when change hits, instead of pausing to ask better questions, you over-function. You power through. You stop listening. Because somewhere along the way, you equated leadership with certainty. And that thought keeps you stuck.

This is the paradox of thoughts: They're quiet, but they're powerful.

Think about Aaron at the end of the table, spinning his pen and smirking through the silence. His sarcastic text later wasn't just a joke; it was the thought loop he had already been playing in his head: *Here we go again, another mess from leadership.* That internal script shaped both his body language in the meeting and the message he sent after it, because thoughts rarely stay private for long; they leak into behavior.

And, like every part of the compass, they can be a strength or a trap.

- **When thoughts are aligned:**
  You think strategically. You process with clarity. You evaluate with intention instead of impulse. This is where your inner logic supports evolution. It helps you lead with direction and discernment.
- **When thoughts are misaligned or distorted:**
  You might overanalyze, get stuck in assumptions, or spiral into negativity disguised as realism. You default to safety in your head and forget to check what's actually true in the room. In other words? You start believing your thoughts without testing them.

Thoughts can empower or entrap.

And because they run so deep, we often confuse them with facts. But thoughts aren't truth. They're just *practice*. The more you think a thought, the more familiar it becomes. Neuroscientist Donald Hebb described this as "what fires together, wires together." His research in 1949 laid the foundation for understanding how repeated thought patterns build strong neural pathways, whether they serve us or not (Hebb, 1949). Your brain builds a fast-track neural loop: *"We've thought this before, it must be right."*

But repetition isn't *proof*. It's just frequency.

And if you're not actively examining the thoughts that drive you, they'll keep driving, without your permission.

This is where reflection becomes critical. Ask yourself:
- What thoughts am I rehearsing on a loop?
- Are they aligned with the kind of leader I want to be?
- Do they serve the moment, or sabotage it?
- Are they rooted in confidence, or in fear disguised as strategy?

One of the most powerful leadership shifts you can make is moving from automatic thought to intentional thought.

That doesn't mean you force toxic positivity. It means you *notice* the narrative before you act on it. You create space between the trigger and the response. You learn to pause long enough to ask, *"Is that actually true, or just familiar?"*

Because once you name a thought, you can challenge it. And once you challenge it, you create space for a new one. And that space? That's where evolution lives.

West: Your Emotions – What You Feel (and Often Hide)

Emotions are the final direction on the Behavior Compass, and they're often the most underestimated.

While values anchor us, beliefs shape our reality, and thoughts build the script... emotions are the accelerant. They determine how fast we react, how loud we speak, and how much of ourselves we're willing to bring into the moment. They don't just influence behavior, they amplify it.

You've seen this play out. You *know* the team values collaboration. You *believe* they're aligned. You've *thought* through the plan. But the moment the announcement drops? Emotions flood the room, and suddenly, nothing's landing the way it should.

That's because behavior is rarely just logical; it's emotional. Even the best plan can unravel if emotions aren't acknowledged. That doesn't mean we let feelings run the show, but we do have to recognize that they're always in the room. Emotions don't need your permission to exist. They just need your attention. If you don't make space for them, they'll show up anyway, just sideways.

That was Tom in the meeting, furiously texting under the table. On the surface, it looked like a distraction. In reality, it was frustration finding a backdoor. He didn't feel safe enough to say it out loud, so his emotions showed up in the only place he felt they could, through his phone. That's how emotions work when ignored. They don't vanish; they leak. That looks like:

- Passive resistance that gets framed as "concern"
- Silence in meetings that's mistaken for alignment
- Eye rolls in the back row while someone's nodding in the front

When people can't say how they feel, they'll show it. And if you're not watching for those signals, you'll miss the moment when engagement quietly exits the room.

Now here's where it connects back to the compass:

- When values are violated, emotions flare.

- When beliefs are challenged, emotions tighten.
- When thoughts spiral, emotions escalate.
- And when all three are out of sync? Emotions take over.

Emotions, just like the other compass points, come with both strength and struggle:

- **When emotions are aligned:**
  You lead with empathy, human connection, motivation, and engagement. You can tune into the emotional energy of a room and adjust your approach without losing your message. That's where influence gets its heartbeat.

- **When emotions are misaligned or unchecked:**
  You may lead from reaction instead of intention. You may become inconsistent, overly sensitive, avoidant, or emotionally numb. And emotional avoidance is just as dangerous as emotional volatility. In both cases, your team ends up confused, and that confusion becomes a breeding ground for disengagement.

This is why emotional intelligence isn't optional. It's the regulator of the entire compass.

So, as a leader, you've got to ask:

- What emotion is driving this reaction?
- Is it grounded in something real, or in a story I haven't named?

- What emotional signals am I picking up (or ignoring)?
- And how do my own emotions shape the space I create for others?

This doesn't mean you need to be a therapist. But it does mean you need to lead with emotional clarity, not emotional confusion, because the more aware you are of the emotional undercurrent, the more effective your leadership will be.

Emotions aren't soft. They're strategic.

When we ignore them, we lose influence. When we name them, we build trust. And trust is what makes real evolution possible.

Behavior Mapping – Connecting the Dots

Now that you've explored all four directions of the Behavior Compass, North: Values, East: Beliefs, South: Thoughts, and West: Emotions, it's time to connect the dots.

Because here's the truth: Behavior doesn't just "happen." It's a product of all four forces working together (or against each other) beneath the surface. And if we want to evolve how we lead, collaborate, or respond to change, we can't just look at what people are *doing*. We need to understand what's *driving* it. Think back to David's meeting. On the surface, you saw silence, crossed arms, and a sarcastic text afterward. But beneath that behavior were values, beliefs, thoughts, and emotions all pulling in different directions. That's exactly what Behavior Mapping helps reveal, the why behind what you see.

That's where Behavior Mapping comes in.

This isn't a personality test or a one-time worksheet. It's a simple framework to pause and ask:

"What's working, what's not, and what's underneath it?"

It's a mental model to keep in your leadership back pocket. You can use it for yourself, with your team, or even in a live coaching moment when things feel off. It brings structure to reflection and gives language to the stuff that usually stays buried. Here is how it works:

Step 1: Identify the Behavior You Want to Understand or Shift

Start with what you're noticing. Is it silence? Defensiveness? Over-functioning? Avoidance? Don't label the person, just describe the pattern or behavior.

What are you noticing? Is it withdrawal? Defensiveness? Over-functioning? Silence in meetings? Frustration during change rollouts?

Choose one. Keep it simple.

Example: "I shut down when my ideas aren't acknowledged."

This step is about *observation*, not judgment. You're not labeling a personality flaw. You're noticing a pattern that shows up in the moment and deserves curiosity, not critique.

Step 2: Map the Current State Using the Compass

Once the behavior is named, move through the Compass. One direction at a time.

Use these prompts to reflect:

- **North: Values**

    Which of my core values feels activated or violated right now? Is there something I care about that's not being seen, honored, or protected?

- **East: Beliefs**

    What belief could be influencing this behavior? Is it true, or just familiar? Did I adopt this belief in a moment of stress, survival, or disappointment?

- **South: Thoughts**

    What's the internal script running in the background? What's the story I'm telling myself right now, and how long has it been playing on loop?

- **West: Emotions**

    What emotion is present beneath the surface? Not just the one I can name quickly, but the one I don't want to admit is there. What's really being felt?

Example Mapping:

- **Value:** Respect – "I want to feel seen and taken seriously."
- **Belief:** "Leaders don't listen unless you're already in the inner circle."
- **Thought:** "Speaking up won't change anything."

- **Emotion:** Frustration sitting on top of disappointment

When you map this out, the behavior that once felt confusing starts to make perfect sense. And that's the power of this work. You stop personalizing and start understanding. You can see the person behind the pattern. And if you're mapping your own behavior, you can offer yourself insight instead of shame.

Step 3: Map the Desired State

Now shift the lens. Imagine you were operating from a more aligned, more grounded state.

What does that version of you (or your team) look like?

- What value do you want to lead from instead?
- What belief would support that version of the moment?
- What thought would offer clarity or possibility?
- What emotion would create energy instead of resistance?

Example Desired Mapping:

- **Value:** Courage – "I speak even when it's uncomfortable."
- **Belief:** "My voice may not change everything, but it always matters."
- **Thought:** "I can bring something valuable to the table."
- **Emotion:** Grounded confidence

The goal here isn't to perform a 180. It's to imagine a more intentional way of responding and give yourself a way to practice it.

Step 4: Reflect on the Gap
Look at your two maps, Current State and Desired State, and ask:
- *What's holding me back from shifting?*
- *What part of my compass needs the most attention right now?*
- *Where could I practice a new behavior in a low-stakes moment?*
- *What would it look like to try a different way, even once?*

You don't need a full mindset transformation to start moving. You just need *awareness + one action.*

That's how new behavior is born.

Why This Works
Behavior Mapping gives you more than a moment of reflection, it gives you a roadmap. One you can use again and again when things feel stuck, unclear, or just... off.

It turns invisible drivers into visible insights. And from there? You get to choose what happens next.

This isn't just a tool for individuals. It's a way for teams to surface tension with more clarity and less blame. For leaders to coach with more precision. For cultures to evolve with more honesty and less spin.

Because when you can name what's underneath the behavior, you can change it without losing what matters most.

And that? That's evolution in real time. You can find the Behavior Mapping worksheet in the back of this book or you can download a printable copy at TheEvolutionaryMindset.com/Tools

Realignment Is the Work of Evolution
The goal isn't perfection. It's alignment.
Not everything in your leadership needs to be fully formed or flawlessly executed. What matters more is whether you're willing to pay attention when something feels off and take steps to realign. That's the real work of evolution.
Because life moves fast. Conversations go sideways. People surprise us. Plans shift. And in the middle of it all, your compass is working quietly, pulling you toward something true, or warning you that something's off.
Realignment doesn't announce itself. It doesn't show up with a motivational playlist or a perfectly color-coded action plan. It happens in the in-between moments. The pause before you hit send. The thought you challenge before it becomes a reaction. The emotion you name before it hijacks the room. The belief you finally admit is outdated, even if it served you once.
That's the practice.
And while it might sound subtle, the impact is anything but. Because when you realign your values, beliefs, thoughts, and emotions, even slightly, you begin to shift your presence. And presence changes everything. It's what allows people to trust

you. To hear you. To follow you even when things are hard, because they sense that you're not leading from ego or fear, you're leading from intention.

This is the kind of leadership that doesn't need noise to be noticed. It shows up in calm rooms and clear decisions. In teams that speak the truth, not just what's safe. In cultures that don't just perform change but embody growth. And it all starts with awareness.

So, if something you read in this chapter stirred something in you, pay attention. If you recognized a behavior you're ready to shift, or a direction on the compass that's been running the show a little too long, good. That's the signal.

You don't have to overhaul everything. You just need to notice where you are, and take one intentional step toward where you want to be. That's not just reflection. That's realignment.

And that's how evolution begins.

Later, in Chapter 10, we'll introduce the Compass Check-In, a tool designed for real-time use when you're in the middle of the moment. Together, these two practices, mapping for reflection and checking in for momentum, create a leadership rhythm that's grounded, responsive, and fully aligned with the Evolutionary Mindset.

One helps you understand. The other helps you act. And both are here to help you lead forward.

Part II
Building the Evolutionary Mindset

Chapter 4

Calibrate the Compass – How Evolution Ready Are You?

A few years ago, our organization made a big shift, one that, on paper, made perfect sense. We centralized all of our employee investigations into a Center of Excellence (COE). It was a smart move. A common best practice in large companies. And it freed up our HR Business Partners to focus on higher-value strategic work.

But here's what the org chart didn't show: the ripple of quiet resistance that followed. Not because people didn't understand the change, but because they felt it before they ever thought it through.

The HRBPs were nervous. The business leaders were uneasy. And it wasn't because the logic was flawed. It was because something deeper was happening beneath the surface: relationships were being redefined. Trust was being redistributed. And emotions were running the show.

I still remember that first rollout meeting. The VP was at the front of the room, walking us through a crisp deck. Flowcharts. Timelines. Boxes inside boxes. It was the kind of presentation that looked like it had been built in PowerPoint's "executive template" setting. Everything clean, polished, logical.

But the room told another story. One HRBP, Natalie, sat with her arms crossed so tight it looked like she was holding herself together. Another, Ryan, kept scrolling on his phone, looking like he was pondering his next job opportunity. Which, everyone knew that he was because almost every day at lunch, he would say something to the effect of, "Hey, did you see that so-n-so is hiring? I think I am going to apply." When the VP asked if there were questions, you could feel the hesitation pressing down like a heavy blanket. No one wanted to go first.

That's the thing about resistance, it doesn't usually show up in bold defiance.

It shows up in silence.

Later that afternoon, a business leader, let's call her Traci, pulled me aside in the hallway. She was sharp, seasoned, and the kind of leader people trusted to get things done. But that day, she looked uneasy. Her voice was steady, but her eyes betrayed her nerves.

"I won't have any use for the COE," she said flatly. "I already have my HR partner."

That wasn't defiance. That was fear. Fear that she'd lose the person she trusted. Fear that the new structure meant she'd be left without a voice or an advocate. Fear that the COE would become just another faceless function instead of a real partner.

I could hear the subtext in her tone: *Don't take away the one person who understands me. Don't make me start over with a stranger.*

And you know what? That's not irrational. Because trust isn't transferable. You can't hand it off like a baton and expect the race to keep its pace. Trust is earned over time, through countless small interactions, late-night calls, tough conversations, and moments when someone went to bat for you. And when people are scared, logic doesn't override emotion. If anything, logic just feels like salt in the wound: "Don't tell me why it makes sense; show me how I can still feel safe."

This is where psychological safety makes or breaks moments. As Amy Edmondson (2019) reminds us, people don't resist change; they resist the loss of voice, connection, and stability that often comes with it. What Marcy voiced in that hallway was the thing everyone else was thinking but didn't dare say out loud.

And here's the kicker: she wasn't wrong to feel it.

The weeks that followed were proof. HRBPs were quieter in meetings, careful with their words, and a little less available than before. Leaders grew tentative, second-guessing whether to bring issues forward. It wasn't mutiny; it was hesitancy. And that's the most dangerous kind of resistance, because it's invisible until it stalls progress.

You can roll out the cleanest strategy, with the sharpest PowerPoint slides and the best intentions, and still watch it falter. Because when mindset isn't aligned, the message doesn't land.

Most organizations spend a lot of time measuring things: performance, engagement, turnover, productivity. We've got dashboards for days. I once saw a company track how many lattes were sold at the café as a proxy for employee satisfaction. Because nothing says "cultural health" like a spike in oat milk usage.

But very few stop to measure what's driving all of it: mindset. And even fewer know how to talk about mindset in a way that feels concrete.

We assume mindset is either fixed or self-evident. That if someone's a high performer, they must have a high-functioning mindset. That if a team's hitting its targets, everything under the surface must be fine. But if the last twenty years in HR have taught me anything, it's this: mindset rarely shows up in the metrics until it becomes a problem.

By the time disengagement shows up in a survey, the mindset has already shifted. By the time turnover spikes, the trust is already broken. And by the time a leader's behavior becomes a liability, the patterns are long established.

That's why mindset matters. And that's why we measure it. Too often, organizations skip straight to execution. But mindset is the filter that every message, decision, and action passes through. If the filter is cloudy, even the best strategy gets distorted.

That's why we need a mirror, not a microscope.

A microscope narrows your vision, forcing you to study a fragment under pressure. A mirror widens your view, forcing you to look at yourself. Mindset work is mirror work. You have to see what's really there, even the parts you'd rather not, before you can adjust.

Mindset isn't something you can fix with a quick training or a better process. You have to see it first. You have to understand how someone's beliefs, emotions, and thought patterns are shaping their experience of change, and their ability to move through it.

Being evolution-ready isn't about resisting change less. It's about visibility. It's about surfacing what's happening underneath so you can lead what's really going on. And that starts by asking: *How equipped is my mindset for evolution?*

This chapter isn't here to hand you a report card. It's here to help you pause, look inward, and ask one of the most important leadership questions you can ask: Where am I calibrated, and where am I off course?

And the answer isn't found in effort. It's found in awareness.

Try This: A Sample Mindset Scan

Before diving into the scan, let's pause here: Mindset isn't about personality. It's about patterns. These five categories aren't random; they reflect the internal GPS guiding your behavior, especially under pressure. The more accurately you can name where you're off course, the more precisely you can correct it.

Before we move forward, let's take a moment to look inward. The following reflection is a brief sample of the full Evolutionary Mindset Assessment. It's not meant to give you a complete diagnostic; it's meant to give you a sense of how your mindset is currently operating. Think of it as a quick gut check, not a final grade.

For each of the five categories below, read the statements and rate how true they feel for you today. Use the following guide:

0 – Rarely or never true
1 – Sometimes true
2 – Often or always true

When you're finished, total the scores in each category. A higher score doesn't mean you've failed; it simply highlights where your mindset may be carrying extra tension or friction. It's your brain's way of asking for support, not your ego's way of asking for validation.

Perception of Reality
- I often react based on what I fear may happen, not what is actually happening.
- I struggle to pause and examine whether my assumptions are rooted in fact.

- I assume people's intentions before I ask for clarification.

Emotional Stamina
- I tend to shut down, get overwhelmed, or default to avoidance when things feel uncertain.
- My emotional triggers often shape my response before I've had time to think.
- I carry the emotional weight of change longer than I want to admit.

Intentional Thinking
- I find myself making fast decisions to relieve discomfort, rather than waiting for clarity.
- I rarely stop to ask, "What do I know to be true?" before moving forward.
- I have a hard time slowing down my thinking once I'm emotionally activated.

Adaptability
- I get stuck in familiar routines, even when they're no longer working.
- When change happens, I tend to wait for others to figure it out before I engage.
- I silently resist change if I wasn't involved in creating it.

Relational Alignment
- My team and I are not always moving in the same direction, even if it looks like we are on the surface.
- I often keep my real concerns to myself, assuming they won't be heard or acted on.
- I sometimes assume people "should just know" how I feel without me saying it directly.

If you scored a three or higher in any one section, that's a signal worth paying attention to. This doesn't mean something's wrong. It means something's "asking" for your attention. Treat it like a dashboard light, not a verdict, but a helpful signal. And the more curious you are, the more insightful this work becomes. Not because something's broken, but because something may be out of sync. This is the moment to shift from autopilot to awareness. The more clearly you can see where your mindset could be off course, the more effectively you can lead forward, with clarity, with confidence, and with less unnecessary resistance.

Mindset isn't fixed. But it does need to be seen before it can be shifted. And now, you're beginning to see it.

Want the Full Picture?
If the sample scan sparked some insight, that's good. But insight is just the beginning.

The full Evolutionary Mindset Assessment is where things get clearer and more actionable. It's a 50-question diagnostic designed to give you a deeper understanding of how your mindset is currently showing up across all five dimensions. Your results aren't just a score. They're a snapshot of what's working, what's holding you back, and where small shifts could create meaningful momentum.

You'll also have the option to generate a team heatmap, a visual tool that shows how your team's mindset is calibrated. Are you aligned? Fragmented? Are you evolving together or just sharing the same org chart? The heatmap helps you spot patterns, surface unspoken dynamics, and have the kinds of conversations that shift culture, not just behavior.

You can access the full assessment, your individual profile, and team tools at **TheEvolutionaryMindset.com/tools**. It's fast, secure, and designed for professionals at every level, from frontline to C-suite.

Because when you see your mindset clearly, you stop reacting from habit and start responding with intention. And that's when evolution really begins.

Chapter 5

Emotional Stamina: The Inner Evolution Engine

Meet Tina.

Tina had made hard calls before. Downsizing. Budget cuts. Reorgs that shifted who reported to whom. But this one landed differently. It wasn't about one individual role or a seasonal fluctuation; it was about closing down an entire department.

On paper, the rationale was airtight. The work had been critical two decades ago, but the business had evolved. The functions were duplicated elsewhere, technology had automated much of the process, and the costs no longer justified the outcomes. Any consultant would have circled it in red ink and highlighted: *opportunity for better efficiency*.

But that wasn't the whole story. The department wasn't just four headcount lines. It was four people who had become woven into the fabric of the company.

Lenard had been there the longest, more than twenty years. He had lived through three CEOs, five software conversions, and more mergers than anyone could count. When leaders came and went, Lenard was the constant. He had the most institutional knowledge, and he was frequently called on to share it. He carried an easy calm that younger employees leaned on when things felt chaotic. "If Lenard's not panicked, we're fine," they used to say.

Mariella was the heart. Her office always smelled faintly of cinnamon tea, and people swore she had a sixth sense for when someone was having a bad day. She remembered birthdays. She kept tissues in her desk drawer. She had a Damn It Doll on her crowded bookshelf full of mementos she would offer to those who needed a safe space to vent. She was the unofficial therapist for half the building and the glue in more ways than one.

Silva was the expert. Precise, sharp, and quietly proud of her encyclopedic knowledge. People joked she knew the company handbook better than the lawyers did. Her advice wasn't flashy, but it was trusted deeply. "If Silva says it's right, it's right." Losing her meant losing not just knowledge but certainty.

And **Carlos**? Carlos was the spark. He had a way of breaking tension with a well-timed quip that made everyone breathe again. He was generous with his time, patient with newer employees, and had a laugh that echoed down the hall. People said meetings weren't the same without him, not just quieter, but heavier.

Tina knew their departure would ripple.

The day of the announcement, she kept rehearsing her words, but nothing felt adequate. She could explain *why*. She could outline efficiencies. She could talk about the future. But she couldn't soften what it meant to lose people like Lenard, Mariella, Silva, and Carlos.

The meeting itself was almost too quiet. No one shouted. No one protested. Instead, people sat still, faces unreadable, as if they were trying to process what this meant for them. Tina felt it in her gut: change doesn't just move boxes on an org chart. It shakes the ground people stand on.

And that was the part no slide deck ever prepared you for.

A week later, Tina saw it play out in the breakroom.

Brandon stood at the sink, rinsing his water bottle. He stared at nothing in particular, lost in thought, while the water kept running. It filled the bottle, spilled over the top, and began pooling on the counter.

"Hey, here, let me help you with that," Megan said, walking in. She grabbed a handful of paper towels and passed some to him, laughing softly as she sopped up the spill.

Brandon blinked, embarrassed. "Guess my head's somewhere else."

"Join the club," Megan said gently. She tossed her soggy towels into the bin and leaned against the counter.

Brandon hesitated, then lowered his voice. "I just can't stop thinking about it. Lenard. Mariella. Silva. Carlos. They gave their whole careers here. If *they* can be let go, then what does that say about the rest of us? No one's safe, right?"

Megan exhaled, pressing fresh towels into the counter. "That's exactly what people are worried about. Nobody's saying it out loud, but everyone's thinking it."

Tina had just walked in, catching enough of the exchange to feel the weight of it. She cleared her throat softly. Both Brandon and Megan straightened, startled.

"I heard what you said," Tina said, choosing her words carefully. "And I don't want to dismiss it. You're right, it's unsettling. Those four weren't just coworkers. They were anchors. And losing them hurts."

The room was silent for a moment. Megan crossed her arms. Brandon looked down at his shoes.

"But here's what I want you to hear," Tina said, her voice steady but warm. "Their departure doesn't erase their value, or yours. The truth is, the work changed. The business changed. But what hasn't changed is how much we rely on you, your ideas, your energy, your commitment, to keep this place moving forward. That matters more now than ever."

Brandon finally lifted his eyes. "It's just... hard to separate the business decision from the personal. They were... well, they were the people we leaned on."

"I know," Tina said softly. "I leaned on them, too. This isn't just a business decision; it's a loss. And I feel it with you. Part of leadership is balancing two truths: what the business requires and what the people experience. I can't make the hard part disappear, but I can promise you this: I'll keep showing up, I'll keep listening, and I'll keep making space for what you're feeling. You don't have to carry this alone."

The room grew quiet again, but this time it felt different. Not fixed. Not resolved. But steadier.

That's what emotional stamina looks like.

It isn't about powering through or pretending the feelings aren't there. It's about being present long enough for people to feel seen in the middle of the disruption. It's about resisting the instinct to fast-forward to metrics and efficiencies and instead holding steady in the discomfort. Months later, the efficiencies did come. Processes smoothed, costs lowered, and the remaining team members moved forward. But Tina knew that the real test wasn't whether the numbers worked. It was whether her people still believed they were standing on solid ground.

And belief like that isn't built through strategy decks. It's built in breakroom conversations, over spilled water bottles, when a leader is willing to stop, acknowledge the weight, and carry it alongside their people.

Because emotional stamina isn't about staying calm. It's about staying with the weight, with the silence, with the people who need to know they're not carrying it alone.

Mirror Moment

What emotion do you find hardest to hold, and what might happen if you stopped trying to manage it and started learning from it?

Change often asks people to let go of more than a role or a routine. Sometimes it asks them to let go of a piece of their identity. And when that happens, your leadership can't just be smart, it has to be steady.

This is where Edmondson's (2019) work on psychological safety rings true, emotions that are suppressed don't disappear; they resurface as resistance. Organizations that lead through emotional truth, not avoidance, retain more trust through transitions.

This chapter is about building that steadiness. Not by shutting emotion down, but by learning to move through it, with clarity, with compassion, and with the kind of consistency that earns trust when everything else feels uncertain. You began that reflection in Chapter 4 with the mini-assessment, but if emotional stamina feels like a growth edge for you, don't stop there. The full Evolutionary Mindset Assessment goes deeper and can give you a clear picture of where your mindset holds steady and where it may still default to protect instead of progress.

Emotional stamina isn't about staying calm. It's about staying present, especially when calm has left the building. It's the skill that lets you sit in the discomfort of uncertainty, disappointment, or pushback without shutting down, lashing out, or spiraling into self-doubt. It's what separates the leaders who can navigate turbulence with steadiness… from the ones who quietly self-combust behind polite smiles and bullet points.

Let's name something out loud: Most of us weren't taught emotional stamina. We were taught how to problem-solve. How to communicate. Maybe even how to lead change. But no one handed us a guidebook on how to stay emotionally grounded when the change you just rolled out hits your team like a wrecking ball… or when your boss drops a "quick pivot" on a Friday at 4:45 p.m.

Some people may chalk that up to experience. "You'll learn emotional resilience the hard way," they say, like it's some rite of passage from the School of Hard Knocks. But if that were true, wouldn't we be better at it by now? There's no shortage of leaders in the world, but there is a shortage of leaders who've been taught how to lead through emotion instead of around it. Emotional stamina isn't something we've prioritized. It's something we've expected people to figure out on their own, usually under pressure, and usually too late. Let me tell you a truth I couldn't see at the time.

Earlier in my career, I was working for a company I still adore to this day. I had a great team, a strong leader, and a rhythm that felt comfortable. Well, we all know that comfort is the enemy of growth. So, my boss challenged me and encouraged me to start thinking about my next step within the organization. When I started considering different options, my boss encouraged me to apply for a new internal role. The catch? It wasn't the role I wanted. The team had growing pains. Their internal brand was rough. And they were operating like a startup inside a well-oiled machine, with lots of potential, but equally, lots of chaos.

I said no. Twice. On the third ask, I yielded. My leader told me it would grow my career faster than anything else I could take. And they were right. I applied. I interviewed. I accepted the role, and I went in kicking and screaming.

What followed was one of the most uncomfortable seasons of my career. The work was meaningful, but I felt like I was on shaky ground every day. I missed my old team. I missed the familiar cues of trust and stability. I second-guessed myself constantly. And if I'm being honest, I didn't show up as my best self every day. It was because I was struggling to find my footing emotionally.

Looking back now, I realize I wasn't failing, I was evolving. But I didn't have the language for it then. My emotional stamina was being tested not by crisis, but by friction. And not because people were doing anything wrong, but because everything was new. New role. New partners. New politics. New dynamics. And new rules I didn't yet understand. My Compass was spinning. My values felt misaligned. My beliefs were being challenged. My thoughts were fogged by doubt. And emotionally, I was trying to muscle through it instead of making sense of it. But I see it clearly now: I wasn't just managing change, I was carrying the emotional weight of a leadership identity shift. And I was doing it without the tools I now teach.

That experience eventually led to a promotion. But it came at a cost. I didn't just grow my career, I stretched my capacity. And I never forgot what that season felt like. It's part of the reason I believe so deeply in this work now. Because when emotional stamina is present, you evolve with intention. When it's missing, you white-knuckle your way through… and call it resilience. That's where emotional stamina comes in. It's not flashy. It doesn't win "most innovative" at the annual leadership summit. But it's the thing that keeps you from burning out, blowing up, or bailing when leadership gets real. As we explored in Chapter 2, your brain isn't built for nuance under pressure; it's built to protect. And when it senses a threat, even if that "threat" is just feedback or silence in a meeting, it triggers reactivity. Emotional stamina is the skill that lets you stay anchored when that protective wiring kicks in. Because here's the truth, most organizations overlook: people aren't resisting the change because they don't understand it. They're resisting because they feel it, and they don't know what to do with that feeling.

Here's where it gets real. I've coached two leaders through nearly identical restructures. One powered through the rollout, 20-minute town hall, bullet points on a slide, no eye contact, and then quickly exited. The other one stuck around after the meeting. She stood in front of the team, looked people in the eye, and said, "I know this is hard. I feel it, too." Same change. Very different aftermath. One team quietly unraveled. The other pulled tighter. The difference wasn't strategy. It was stamina.

But we still tell ourselves the old lies: Emotions don't belong in business. If I acknowledge how people feel, I'll make it worse. If I let emotion into the room, I'll lose control. None of that is true. In fact, the opposite is true. Emotional avoidance doesn't keep things clean; it makes things corrosive. And silence is rarely a strategy. It's just the place where resentment goes to fester.

Where do most leaders get stuck? They over-explain to dodge discomfort. They mistake "professional" for "distant." They think their job is to fix, instead of feel. And they confuse alignment with agreement, when really what they're getting is compliance without connection.

Emotional stamina doesn't thrive in a vacuum. It thrives on trust. And when trust is missing, showing up with emotional presence is a heavier lift because instead of grounded vulnerability, what you're navigating is *guarded survival*. That doesn't mean emotional stamina isn't possible in low-trust environments. It means leaders carry more weight to create the conditions where safety can grow again.

So, what's your responsibility when trust is fractured?

Not to fake calm. Not to skip to strategy. But to acknowledge what's real without making it worse. To be steady, not slick. To say, "This is hard and I am here," instead of rushing to prove your point or fix what people haven't even finished feeling yet.

When teams are low on trust, emotional stamina isn't just a leadership tool; it's a test. And it doesn't show up in performance reviews or a dashboard. But over time, it shows up in engagement scores, retention data, and whether your top talent chooses to stay when things get hard. It shows up in whether people brace themselves when you speak… or breathe.

The truth is, emotional stamina is a competitive advantage. The leaders who build it don't just survive change; they make others braver in the face of it. They normalize discomfort without dramatizing it. They let people feel what they need to feel without letting feelings drive the car. And when emotions are in the driver's seat, they rarely act alone. As we unpacked in Chapter 3, the Behavior Compass, your values, beliefs, thoughts and emotions work as a system. When one point is activated, the others often follow. Emotional stamina helps you name what's being triggered before you spiral into reaction. That kind of leadership shifts everything.

In the chapters that follow, we'll break this down. We'll explore how discomfort gets misread as danger. We'll look at emotional triggers, those moments where your past hijacks your present, and how to pause before reacting. We'll learn how to move from impulse to intention. And we'll close with the most underused leadership muscle of all: consistency.

This isn't a detour from leadership. This is the heart of it. If you want to lead a team through the hard stuff, you don't need more control. You need more capacity. And that starts here.

Chapter 6

Discomfort: Fear-Based Resistance vs. Emotion-Driven Momentum

When I was seven or eight, we moved to a new city. Not just across town, out of state. Far from family. Far from friends. Far from anything that felt familiar. At that age, you don't think of it as "a new chapter." You feel it in your stomach as the quiet panic of being the new kid who doesn't know where to sit at lunch.

My mom, trying to help me adjust, asked me if I wanted to sign up for a sport. She offered the typical list: soccer, softball, maybe swimming lessons. But I had an idea lodged in my head. "I want to twirl a baton," I told her.

She didn't push back or try to redirect me to something more popular or practical. She just said, "Okay," and signed me up. I'll never forget walking into that massive gym for the first time. The ceilings stretched impossibly high, and every sound seemed to bounce off them, batons clattering to the floor, sneakers squeaking, coaches clapping out counts. All around me, girls were tossing batons skyward, spinning underneath them, catching with precision, and rolling straight into their next trick. They were practicing for an upcoming competition, their hair slicked back into tight buns, their leotards sequined in every color imaginable. The whole room glittered. To me, as a little girl, it was mesmerizing. These girls looked effortless. Confident. Like they belonged. I stood there frozen, equal parts intimidated and inspired, thinking: *I want to be like that.* From then on, I practiced constantly. After school, I'd run to the backyard with my practice baton and spin until my arms were covered in constant bruises from trying desperately to catch the tiny silver bar. I dropped it more times than I can count, leaving dents in the grass. My wrists were bruised, my hands sore, but I kept going. I'd close my eyes and picture myself in one of those glittering costumes, part of the line of girls who looked like they had mastered the secret.

Then came Parents' Day.

The gym was full. Moms and dads leaning forward with cameras, ready to capture their child's big moment. Girls were clustered into their different age groups, going through their tricks and routines. My mom looked for me in the group. But I wasn't there.

I was off to the side. Alone. Not included.

My mom frowned and asked why.

The gym owner's response came quick, almost casual: "Amy has no rhythm. She struggles with hand-eye coordination. She'll never be good at this. She should try something else, maybe soccer or music. This just isn't for her."

I was standing right there.

The words sliced through me. My face went hot, my stomach dropped. I felt exposed, like my failure had been announced over a loudspeaker. At that age, you don't know how to put it in perspective. You don't think, *She doesn't know what she's talking about.* You think, *She must be right. Something's wrong with me.*

That moment could have defined me. And for a while, it almost did.

Because here's what discomfort feels like when you're a child: it feels final. It doesn't register as a challenge you can push through. It registers as danger. My body locked up. My mind raced. *I just want to go home.*

But my mom wouldn't let that be the end of the story. That night, she sat with me in my bed, stroking my head to comfort me. She let me cry. She didn't rush me or say "Don't let it get to you." She sat in it with me. And when the tears slowed, she said, "You don't have to stop trying. You just need a different place to try."

And then she did something brave. She signed me up for dance classes. I had been dancing for a couple of years before the move, and it was familiar to me. But this feeling of rejection and shame wasn't.

I resisted. Hard. I was certain the same thing would happen again. New gym. New teacher. New group of girls. Same humiliation. My fear wasn't nerves; it was certainty. *I will fail again. I will be told, again, that I am not enough.*

But my mom nudged me forward, and I showed up. She said, "You have to get back up and try again."

The first classes weren't easy. I was completely in my head and so distracted by what everyone might be thinking about me, I found myself not thinking about the class. I stumbled. I missed counts. I turned the wrong direction. Every mistake sent heat to my cheeks, the old shame threatening to flare. But this time, the teacher didn't dismiss me. She corrected me. Encouraged me. She said things like, "Everyone starts here. Just keep going."

And I did. Class after class, step by step, the fear loosened. The baton gym memory didn't vanish, but it stopped running the show. Little by little, I started to believe in myself again. Fast forward twenty years. I danced professionally until I was thirty. I was never the star of the room, but I belonged. Dance gave me freedom. It gave me a way to express emotions I couldn't always put into words. That little girl's dream of wearing a sparkly costume and being part of something? I got there. Just not the way that baton coach predicted.

That's the power of discomfort. Left unchecked, it shrinks your world. But when you face it with support, honesty, and just enough courage to walk back into the room, it can become the very thing that launches you forward.

I share this story because it shaped something foundational in me. That moment in the gym could have broken my spirit. But instead of letting fear drive the outcome, I chose to let my emotions move me forward. And I couldn't have done it alone. Because sometimes, even as adults, we need someone who sees our potential when we're too wounded to see it ourselves.

What happened in that gym isn't just a childhood memory; it's a pattern I see play out in organizations every day. Discomfort shows up at work looking a lot like danger. People pull back. They go quiet in meetings. They avoid new tools, new roles, new expectations, not because they're incapable, but because somewhere along the line, they learned that missteps equal humiliation. What looks like resistance is often just the nervous system doing its job, confusing discomfort with danger. And here's the leadership challenge: if we don't know how to spot that difference, we write people off too quickly. We label them "not ready," "not a fit," or "never going to get it," when in reality, they might just need what I needed - support, belief, and the space to keep showing up until discomfort turns into momentum.

You will face moments that feel like rejection, failure, or shame. And when you do, you'll have a choice: freeze in fear or move forward with intention. One will shrink you. The other will evolve you. Choose wisely.

Mirror Moment
Where are you mistaking discomfort for danger, and what growth could be waiting if you moved forward anyway?

And here's the full-circle moment.

Thirty-five years later, my daughter asked to take baton lessons. We were living in a different state, and I signed her up at a local gym. One afternoon, while chatting with the Director, I learned something unexpected: she was the daughter of the woman who had told my mom I'd never be good enough.

I didn't say anything. It wouldn't have changed anything. And honestly? I could tell she'd probably used her own emotions to fuel her path, too. Because that's the thing: emotionally driven momentum, when channeled with intention, can shape something powerful.

What I didn't realize then, but see so clearly now, is that discomfort doesn't disappear when we grow up. It just puts on a badge and walks into work with us. And in most workplaces, it gets a bad rap. It's labeled as resistance, dismissed as overreaction, or simply ignored until it shows up as turnover. But discomfort is a messenger, not a menace. Most resistance in change efforts isn't about a lack of willingness, it's about a lack of safety. When people don't feel safe, they can't stretch. Their nervous system is scanning for threats, and anything unfamiliar feels like a risk, no matter how exciting on paper.

Back in Chapter 2, we talked about how the brain's primary job is protection. It doesn't pause to weigh pros and cons or run a cost-benefit analysis. It simply asks, *"Is this safe?"* When the answer is unclear, it slams on the brakes. That wiring hasn't changed since the days when uncertainty meant real danger, and it shows up in our workplaces every day. Leaders often misinterpret what they're seeing. A quiet room. Delays. Disengagement. Odd fixation on details that don't really matter. It looks like negativity or apathy, but more often than not, it's anxiety. It's not defiance. It's defense.

When discomfort strikes, it's usually because something deeper is being triggered. A belief is being challenged. An emotion hasn't been named. A sense of identity is being threatened. This is where the Compass becomes useful again, it helps us recognize that discomfort is rarely random. It's a signal. And the key isn't to push people harder or shame them into compliance. It's to pause long enough to interpret the signal and understand what's really happening beneath the surface.

There is a big difference between danger and discomfort, but our wiring doesn't always know how to tell the difference. So when people pull back, they're not necessarily resisting the change itself. They're trying to protect themselves. Fear-based resistance doesn't usually sound like, *"I hate this plan."* It sounds more like, *"Why are we doing this now?"* or *"What happens to my role?"* And sometimes, it sounds like nothing at all. Silence can be one of the clearest indicators that people feel unsafe.

I once worked with a leadership team rolling out a new enterprise system. On paper, it was an obvious business win: faster access to data, better integration, streamlined communication. Headquarters couldn't understand why the field leaders were dragging their feet. The system solved real problems, so to them, slow adoption looked like stubbornness. The label came quickly: *"They're just stuck in the old way."*

But when we slowed down and used the four guiding questions you read about in Chapter 4: *For what purpose? What do we know to be true? What's the worst that could happen? What is our role?* A different picture started to emerge. The field leaders weren't resisting the system itself. They were resisting what it represented: more central control, less autonomy, and the possibility that the expertise they had built over years, relationships, workarounds, and practical wisdom, was being phased out. The change wasn't technical. It was personal. The issue wasn't functionality. It was fear of becoming obsolete. Once that fear was named, the corporate team could stop trying to "fix" the rollout and start listening to the reality behind the friction. They shifted their approach. Instead of telling the field what would happen, they invited them into co-design. They gave them a real voice in how the tool was implemented. And little by little, momentum returned. Not because the technology changed, but because the mindset did. Fear doesn't always storm into the room waving a red flag. More often, it slips in quietly, through sarcasm, through deflection, or through that uncomfortable silence where everyone nods but no one is actually bought in. If we don't recognize that, we end up leading the wrong conversation. It doesn't matter how many decks you send if you're not tuning into the human experience underneath. Because discomfort left unspoken doesn't disappear, it hardens. And the longer it goes unnamed, the more it calcifies into cynicism, apathy, or passive sabotage. Think of it like a trail in the meadow that gets walked again and again until it becomes a trench. A canyon. A default path the brain follows even when it leads nowhere.

But discomfort isn't the enemy. In fact, it's where momentum begins, if you know how to work with it.

Emotion-driven momentum happens when leaders create a container for discomfort instead of rushing to resolve it. It's what happens when someone says, "I know this is hard, and I'm not going anywhere," instead of pretending everything's fine. It's not about managing emotion. It's about meeting it. One executive I coached, we'll call her Nora, had a habit of fast-forwarding through her team's reactions. She was a very stoic individual and highly analytical. The moment anyone hesitated or questioned a direction, she would push ahead with logic and numbers. No feelings allowed here. To her, the strategy made sense on paper: clear goals, measurable outcomes, no wasted time, but the impact was not what she thought. At first, the signals were subtle. Meetings that had once been animated became increasingly quiet. Direct reports who used to debate ideas now nodded along without much to add. The silence was easy to mistake for alignment, and Nora did. What she didn't see was that her team was retreating. The first undeniable sign came in the employee survey. Scores around psychological safety, communication, and trust in leadership dropped sharply. The written comments were even more telling. "Decisions feel predetermined." "It doesn't matter what we say." "Concerns go nowhere." For a team that had once been vocal and engaged, the shift was stark. When Nora and I sat down to review the results, she was composed, but her frustration was clear.

"I don't get it," she said, sliding the report across the table. "We're hitting our targets. The strategy is solid. Why does it feel like they're slipping away from me?"

"Let's slow it down," I suggested. "Walk me through what happens in your meetings when someone raises a concern." Nora thought for a moment. "I acknowledge it, but I don't linger. If we stay in debate too long, we lose momentum. My job is to keep us moving."

That response opened the door for us to walk through the four guiding questions.

The first question, *"For what purpose?"* stopped her. "The purpose behind moving fast is to keep focus. We don't have the luxury of time this quarter," she said quickly. Then she leaned back, considering. "And if I'm honest, it also keeps things from spiraling. If we let every concern run its course, we'd never make a decision. Speed keeps us from getting stuck." She paused again, quieter this time. "It also feels safer for me. If I keep things moving, there's less room for doubt and complaining."

The second question, *"What do we know to be true?"* brought us back to the survey. Nora studied the scores in silence. "They're disengaged," she finally said. "They don't think I'm listening. I thought I was giving them clarity. What I've really given them is no room to speak."

When we reached the third question, *"What's the worst that could happen?"* she initially brushed it off. "Worst case, we waste time." I let the silence hang, and she sighed. "No. That's not it. The worst case is they stop trusting me. They stop telling me the truth, and I don't see the cracks until it's too late."

The final question, *"What is our role?"* shifted the conversation. "Your role isn't to remove every ounce of discomfort," I said. "It's to hold the space where people can bring it." Nora nodded, almost to herself. "So, my job isn't to shield them from doubt. It's to sit in it with them."

The next week, she tested that idea. In a leadership meeting, one of her directors, Sam, started to voice a concern and then hesitated. Normally, Nora would have jumped in with data to fill the gap, but this time she leaned forward.

"You stopped there," she said. "What's on your mind?"

Sam hesitated again, glancing around the table. "I'm worried the regional plan looks good here, but the rollout will bury the field teams. We don't have the staffing."

The old Nora would have countered with projections and a reminder of the efficiencies the system would bring. Instead, she let the pause stretch. "Tell me more," she said.

The room shifted. Other leaders chimed in, adding concerns that had been sitting under the surface. The conversation was uncomfortable, but for the first time in months, it was real.

Later, Nora reflected on the experience. "I thought efficiency was progress," she said. "Turns out progress is when people trust the room enough to tell me what they're really thinking."

It wasn't a dramatic overnight turnaround, but the shift was unmistakable. Over time, her team's energy began to return. Concerns surfaced earlier, when they could still be addressed. People spoke with more candor. And Nora discovered what every seasoned leader eventually has to face: moving fast isn't the same as moving forward.

From that point forward, she started showing up differently. She didn't slow down her pace, but she began to create intentional pauses. She opened meetings with check-ins. She invited feedback even when it was uncomfortable. She stopped interpreting silence as agreement. And when someone did speak up, she resisted the urge to fix it in real-time. Instead, she listened.

She didn't apologize for the direction, but she acknowledged the weight of the journey. And her team felt that. Slowly, trust returned. Momentum returned. Emotionally driven momentum wasn't just a concept anymore; it was the undercurrent of a team that had found its footing again.

The teams that evolve through change don't have less emotion; they have more language for it. They don't silence discomfort; they sit with it until they understand what's underneath. And because of that, they move faster. Not because they force progress, but because they've cleared the emotional static that slows everything down.

This is the Evolutionary Mindset in action.

As a leader, your job isn't to eliminate discomfort. It's to interpret it. To normalize it. And to help your team move through it instead of getting stuck beneath it.

Common Signs of Fear-Based Resistance

Here are some of the most common signs of fear-based resistance. They're often mistaken for performance issues or disengagement, but they're actually signals:

- Quiet meetings with minimal input, people fear saying the wrong thing.
- Passive compliance, nodding but not following through.
- Gossip and hallway conversations, emotions looking for a safer outlet.
- Hyperfocus on details, small distractions to avoid big uncertainty.

These aren't signs of dysfunction. They're signs of fear. And they require a different kind of leadership. Not more pressure, more presence. Here's the reframe: discomfort isn't a red flag. It's a readiness signal. It means people care. It means the stakes are real. And when you meet discomfort with steady leadership, emotional clarity, and just a little bit of courage? That's when fear-based resistance gives way to something better.

Momentum.

Discomfort is not your enemy. It's your indicator. It's the point where evolution begins, not through force, but through clarity.

Next up: we'll explore the emotional tripwires that hijack that momentum, your triggers. Because before you can lead others through their discomfort, you've got to understand your own.

Chapter 7

Triggers: Understanding the Story You Tell Yourself

Some reactions feel bigger than the moment: a piece of feedback that haunts you all week; a teammate's tone that rubs you wrong before you've had your first cup of coffee; a calendar invite from your boss that simply says "touch base", and suddenly your chest tightens and your brain starts rehearsing worst-case scenarios. Or maybe, like me, you find yourself power-cleaning your house at 8 p.m. on a Tuesday or rage-purging the storage closet because it's the one thing you can control. (Am I the only one that does this?) These aren't overreactions. They're signals. And most of the time, they're not about the moment; they're about the *story* the moment activates.

That story isn't random. It comes from somewhere deep, your values, your beliefs, your thoughts, your emotions. Sound familiar? It should. That's your Behavior Compass in action. A trigger is like a live wire that sets off one or more points on the compass all at once. Your values get challenged, your beliefs get questioned, your thoughts start spiraling, and your emotions jump behind the wheel. And just like that, your internal GPS, which usually helps you lead with intention, starts recalculating based on fear, not facts.

Here's the kicker: Most of us don't even realize it's happening. We just feel the adrenaline spike or the sudden withdrawal or the urge to micromanage and think, "Why am I acting like this?" But if you slow the moment down and trace it through your internal compass, you'll usually find the real reason. That email didn't just annoy you, it poked your belief that your voice doesn't matter. That decision didn't just frustrate you, it threatened your value of autonomy. That silence in the meeting didn't just feel awkward, it activated your fear that you don't belong.

Triggers are personal, patterned, and powerful. But they're not permanent. When we learn to recognize what part of the compass they're lighting up, and why, we get our agency back. We shift from reaction to reflection. From emotional hijack to emotional maturity. From accepting the first version of the story as fact… to editing it with intention. And that's where real leadership begins.

The moment something triggers us, our brain doesn't ask for facts; it makes assumptions. Fast ones. It fills in the blanks with whatever it already believes to be true. Past experiences. Unspoken fears. That one time you were shut down in a meeting and decided it wasn't worth speaking up again. Suddenly, you're not just reacting to the moment, you're reacting to the meaning your brain has assigned to it. And remember from earlier? Your brain's not trying to be difficult. It's doing its job: protect, preserve, repeat. It doesn't care if the story is accurate; it cares if it keeps you safe. So, it leans on old wiring: "Danger. Back away. Don't trust this." That meaning becomes the story. And here's where it gets tricky:

the story feels *true*. It sounds like, "They don't value me," or "If I don't fix this, it's all going to fall apart." But just because the story feels real doesn't mean it *is* real. Most of the time, it's not about what happened, it's about what it *represents*.

Status Quo Bias: "It's Fine. Everything Is Fine."
Status quo bias is sneaky because it does not announce itself with resistance or defiance. It usually shows up as loyalty, or at least what looks like loyalty. It is the brain's way of saying, "Let's stick with the mess we know." Even when the current process is clunky or outdated, the familiarity feels safer than the unknown. As the old saying goes, most people prefer the devil they know to the devil they do not.

We saw this in Jen's story back in Chapter 1. Every time she saw an email titled "Business Update," her chest tightened before she even opened it. The details almost didn't matter. Her brain had already linked that phrase with disruption. Even if the new direction could have been better, her body braced for the familiar pattern of stress and fear. To Jen, the status quo bias wasn't about liking the old way. It was about anticipating what the old signals had always meant: brace yourself, things are about to get messy.

I saw the same thing with a team that spent six months clinging to an outdated reporting structure long after the organization had moved on. On paper, the change was clear. The chart had shifted. The boxes had been redrawn. But for the people in that group, the issue wasn't a matter of structure; it was a matter of safety. They didn't want to let go of the leader who had always advocated for them. Their loyalty was really fear dressed up as rationale. They weren't fighting the new system; they were fighting the uncertainty of whether the new relationships would offer the same trust. Nora, the seasoned executive we met earlier, experienced another version of this. When her team stopped offering feedback in meetings, she initially thought they were aligned. What was really happening was the status quo bias in silence. People had stopped raising concerns not because they didn't care, but because they had convinced themselves it was safer to stay quiet. Silence became the familiar posture. And in a strange way, it became the status quo.

Decades ago, psychologists William Samuelson and Richard Zeckhauser published research in the *Journal of Risk and Uncertainty* showing that people consistently favored the status quo, even when better alternatives were available. They called it 'status quo bias,' and the pattern has shown up in every domain from personal finance to organizational life. Later, John Jost's system justification research showed that people often defend existing systems not because they are fair or efficient, but because defending the familiar feels safer than questioning it. Amy Edmondson, in her book *The Fearless Organization*, makes the point that people rarely resist the mechanics of change itself. What they resist is the loss of voice, stability, and connection that often comes with it. In other words, it is not the new system they fear; it is what might disappear if they let go of the old one.

You will hear status quo bias leak into conversations in familiar ways:

"But this is how we have always done it."

"What if we change it and it makes things worse?"

"Can't we just tweak the old way instead of starting over?"

"It is Mary's decision at the end of the day, so why can't I just go to her instead of my new boss?"

"This doesn't feel like the same company anymore."

On the surface, these comments sound practical, even responsible. But beneath them is a deeper fear: if we let go of what we know, what anchors us? And this is where leadership matters most. The right move is rarely to argue harder with logic. The right move is to pause, step back into the Behavior Compass from Chapter 3, and ask: What values are being pressed here? What beliefs are being questioned? What emotions are flaring? Which thoughts are looping underneath the surface?

When leaders slow down to ask those questions, they give their teams something more powerful than a new chart or process. They give them the courage to redraw the lines. To see that what feels familiar is not always what is best. And that courage is what loosens the grip of the status quo.

Mirror Moment

What am I holding onto that no longer serves me, yet still feels safer than releasing it?

Loss Aversion: "What Might I Lose If This Goes Wrong?"

Loss aversion does not simply make us cautious; it makes us cling. It convinces us that the possibility of losing something, whether that is time, influence, credibility, or control, is far more dangerous than the possibility of gaining something better. Psychologists Daniel Kahneman and Amos Tversky identified this in their research on prospect theory, showing that, in their words, "losses loom larger than gains." Our brains are wired to feel the pain of losing twice as strongly as the satisfaction of winning.

I once coached a senior leader who insisted she was not against adopting a new digital platform. She said she simply did not see the point in being an early adopter. On the surface, that sounded reasonable. Yet as we explored further, it became clear that the platform itself was not the true barrier. Her resistance was tied to identity. She had built her reputation as the go-to person for the current system. People sought her out for answers, and she carried that credibility with pride. The new platform threatened to erase that expertise. Her concern was not about the effort of learning a new tool, but about losing the standing that had defined her role.

Jen felt the weight of loss aversion in a different way. Each time a "Business Update" email appeared in her inbox, she braced before she even opened it. She did not need the details to know something was shifting. To her, those announcements were not simply about new directions. They represented the potential loss of stability, predictability, and the sense that her role was secure. The words in the message mattered less than the subtraction her mind associated with them.

Loss aversion bias is what keeps us holding on to routines, habits, or roles that once gave us pride, even when they no longer serve us well. It convinces us that maintaining the old way is safer, even if the evidence points in a new direction. You hear it surface in conversations that sound cautious rather than resistant, with people saying things like, "I have already invested too much time in this to stop now," or "If we change this, who will come to me anymore," or "I cannot afford to lose momentum," or "What if this makes my role less relevant."

On the surface those statements sound practical. Beneath the surface they reveal fear of loss disguised as pragmatism. The paradox of loss aversion is that the tighter we cling to what is familiar, the more likely we are to lose the very influence, credibility, or control we are trying to protect.

The leadership move is not to oversell the benefits of the new platform or to pretend that transition will be painless. The move is to name what is being protected. To remind people that their expertise, their voice, and their contribution are not being erased, they are evolving. Growth often requires releasing one grip in order to strengthen another, and leaders can help people see that letting go is not the same as losing. This bias shows up in questions like:

- "Where does that leave me?"
- "Will my team still need me if I let this go?"
- "If I speak up now, what might I lose later?"

Mirror Moment

Am I afraid of the change itself, or afraid of what I might lose if it works?

Confirmation Bias: "I Knew It. This Always Happens."

If status quo bias keeps us stuck, and loss aversion keeps us scared, confirmation bias keeps us convinced. It is the brain's favorite shortcut, scanning for evidence that supports what we already believe and filtering out what does not. Daniel

Kahneman described this as part of our reliance on heuristics, the mental shortcuts that simplify complex situations but often distort reality. Under stress, our minds become expert investigators, but only for the story we are already telling ourselves.

I once facilitated a team feedback session where a senior leader received overwhelmingly positive comments, with only one piece of constructive criticism in the mix. Instead of celebrating the 95 percent of feedback that praised her leadership, she fixated on the single critical remark. She waved off the rest and said, "See? This proves I'm not cut out for this role." Her brain only had space for the data point that confirmed her fear.

That is how confirmation bias works. If you believe people do not value your input, you will notice every time someone cuts you off in a meeting. If you think leadership does not really want feedback, every awkward pause or delayed reply becomes proof. The rest gets ignored, minimized, or rationalized away.

Confirmation bias is not limited to individuals. In teams, it often takes the shape of groupthink. One influential person voices an opinion, and the rest of the group unconsciously begins scanning for evidence that supports it while ignoring what does not. What looks like quick alignment is often just shared bias. The danger is that groupthink can feel efficient, but it narrows the field of vision and silences alternative perspectives. Without psychological safety, teams mistake consensus for clarity, and critical information never makes it to the table.

The danger here is not only in what we notice, it is in what we miss. Opportunities for growth. Signs of support. Signals of trust. When our minds are busy collecting evidence for the story we have already decided is true, the other storylines never make it to the surface.

Each of these biases has the same goal: protection. They do not show up because we are difficult or closed-minded. They show up because we are human. Our brains crave safety, certainty, and control. So when something triggers discomfort, these shortcuts activate. They tether us to what is familiar through status quo bias, they keep us focused on what we might lose through loss aversion, and they lock us into the stories we already believe through confirmation bias. Left unchecked, they shape not only our reactions but also our relationships, our decisions, and our leadership presence.

And here is where it gets deeper. We have been taught that feeling doubt, frustration, or fear is a problem. That strong leadership means pushing past discomfort rather than pausing inside it. But what if those uncomfortable feelings are not the problem at all? What if they are the doorway?

That is where we are headed next.

Mirror Moment

What story have I already decided is true, and what might I be filtering out just to keep believing it?

We've been taught feelings are...bad

Meet Claire.

It was her first week on the strategy team, and she was determined to make a good impression. After years of proving herself in another division, she had been offered this promotion with the promise of broader responsibility and greater visibility. She had walked into the building that morning energized, notebook in hand, ready to absorb everything. So, when a few colleagues invited her to join them for lunch, she felt a wave of relief. It was her first chance to meet the team outside of the polished, slightly stiff setting of the 4th floor.

The cafeteria was bustling, trays clattering, conversations layered one over another. Claire balanced her salad and water bottle, scanning the room until she spotted the group sitting in a sun-drenched table near the corner of the room. Kevin was waving her over. She began weaving her way toward them, catching fragments of conversation as she drew near.

"...Blake, you know better than to bring feelings into a conversation with Marco, unless you want to get cut off at the knees."

The remark hung in the air for a moment before it dissolved into nervous laughter. Claire hesitated just long enough to wonder if she had misheard. By the time she reached the table, the others had fallen into a kind of hush, shifting their attention back to their food.

Sliding into an open seat, Claire smiled and said lightly, "Sorry, I think I just caught the end of something. What was that about Marco? Are there any pointers you can share?"

The woman beside her, a soft-spoken analyst named Elena, exchanged a quick glance with the others before leaning closer. "You'll figure it out soon enough, but it's probably better you hear it now. Marco is brilliant, there's no doubt about that. He can deconstruct a business model in minutes", said Elana. Riley spoke up, "I think he must have a photographic memory because he can recall data we discussed a year ago." But when it comes to feelings..."

Elena shook her head slowly, as though words could not quite capture it. "They don't belong in his meetings. Not frustration, not uncertainty, not even enthusiasm if it gets too personal. If you try to name what something feels like, he'll shut you down before you finish your sentence.

Across the table, Jason set down his fork with a dry laugh. "I once admitted I was concerned about the pressure my team was under. He stopped me mid-sentence and said, 'If you want therapy, get a therapist. I hired you to lead, stick to the facts.' The room went silent. "I've never made that mistake again."

Raj, a senior project manager, leaned in as well. "It's not only that he dismisses it. It's the way he makes you feel for even bringing it up. Like you broke an unspoken rule, and now you're the naïve one in the room."

Claire listened, her appetite fading as the weight of their words settled in. She asked quietly, "So what do you all do when you're frustrated or worried about a project? Do you just… keep it to yourselves?"

Raj gave a wry smile. "Pretty much. You save those conversations for lunches like this, or for the walk to the parking lot at the end of the day. But not in front of Marco. He calls it being professional. We call it survival."

As the group continued eating, they traded examples that carried a mix of humor and resignation. Marco brushing off burnout with the words, "Everyone is tired, you need to just move past it." Marco rolling his eyes when someone admitted confusion about a new initiative. Marco praising data delivered with clinical precision, while ignoring the team member who pointed out that morale was quietly eroding. The stories piled up until Claire no longer wondered if the warning was exaggerated. This was the culture she had just stepped into, and the rules were clear.

By the time the group stood to leave the cafeteria, gathering trays and empty cups, the energy had shifted. The easy banter of a lunch break gave way to the quiet anticipation of the meeting ahead. As they walked down the hallway together, Claire felt the mixture of nerves and curiosity that comes with being new. She had admired Marco from afar and had been excited to learn from him. Yet now, with her teammates' words echoing in her ears, she could not help but wonder what it would mean to work under a leader who treated emotions as contraband.

That is the cost of believing that bad feelings are bad. The emotions in Marco's team had not disappeared; they had simply gone underground. They were whispered about at lunch tables, disguised as sarcasm, or carried silently into meetings as disengagement.

You have probably seen Pixar's *Inside Out*. Adults often admit it hit them harder than it hit their kids. At the beginning of the film, Riley is steered almost entirely by Joy, the upbeat emotion desperate to keep everything light and happy. But when real change hits, new school, new city, new everything, Joy's relentless optimism stops working. What saves Riley in the end is not more cheer, it is Sadness. Sadness is what helps Riley ask for help, reconnect with her parents, and tell the truth. And that shift is what allows things to begin healing. The lesson is simple but profound. "Negative" emotions are not negative. They are necessary. They carry information.

They show us what matters, what feels off, and what needs to be named. They help us course correct, not by fixing things immediately, but by clarifying what is real.

In your leadership, sadness might not look like tears. It might look like a team member going quiet in meetings, or a usually upbeat colleague withdrawing. Anger might not look like shouting. It might show up in short emails, clipped replies, or chronic defensiveness. Emotions are not always loud, but they are always in the room. And when leaders teach teams to dismiss those emotions as unproductive, the emotions do not disappear. They just shift underground, where they drain energy instead of informing growth.

With this in mind, here is a reframe worth holding onto:

- Pain can lead to purpose.
- Discomfort can lead to innovation.
- Sadness can lead to connection.

None of those feelings are a problem. In fact, they may be the most honest part of your leadership.

Mirror Moment

What emotion have you been taught to downplay or dismiss, at work, at home, or in leadership?

And what might it be trying to tell you now?

The Anatomy of a Trigger

It's 1:45 p.m., and on her desk is the leftover Starbucks cup from this morning with the half-eaten bacon, Gouda sandwich she shouldn't have eaten. She instantly regretted the decision and knew she should have gotten the healthier egg bites, but they just don't taste as good. I'll try to eat cleaner tomorrow. Again. She thought. On the wall of her cube is the photo holiday card she had made this year for friends and family. She found the unopened card handing off the corner of Ben's desk, who sits 3 cubes in front of her. After the holiday season, Ben transferred to another department and left it there after packing up his desk, so she took it back. She never really liked him much anyway. The photo hangs above a plant that she has named Gloria; it seems to be the only thing thriving under the fluorescent lights.

After lunch, Claire walked with the team toward the conference room. The hallway chatter was light, but she noticed how the energy shifted as they got closer. Voices grew quieter and footsteps quickened, as though everyone was mentally bracing. Claire carried the warnings from lunch in the back of her mind, the reminder never to bring feelings into a conversation with Marco, but she had not yet seen for herself what they meant. Part of her wondered if perhaps her new colleagues had exaggerated, that maybe Marco's reputation was harsher than the reality. She was heeding their warnings, but also was going in with an open mind and ready to give Marco a fair chance.

Inside the conference room, everything seemed ordinary. Laptops were open, coffee cups sat on the table, and pens scratched across paper as people settled in. Marco sat at the head of the table, calm and composed, flipping through slides with the sharp focus Claire had admired from a distance. She had been eager to learn from him, and for a moment she thought perhaps the warnings had been overstated.

The meeting began smoothly. Updates were shared, timelines reviewed. Marco listened, asked precise questions, and moved the conversation forward with efficiency. To Claire, it felt balanced and professional. She did not sense the tension her teammates had described, at least not yet.

Halfway through, Marco opened the floor for ideas on a new client strategy. A pause followed, the kind of silence that stretches a little too long. Claire felt her pulse quicken. She glanced around the room, and the team sat, tight-lipped and avoiding eye contact. She remembered the caution from lunch, but she also knew she had been brought onto this team to contribute. Choosing her words carefully, she offered a suggestion from her previous division.

"In my last role, we faced a similar challenge," she said, her tone steady but cautious, "and what worked for us was creating a cross-functional review early in the process. It helped us catch problems before they grew."

A few heads turned toward her. For a moment, she thought her idea might gain traction. She looked back at Marco, waiting for his response.

He did not look up from his slides. "We tried that two years ago and it didn't work." His tone was flat and final, as if the matter had already been decided.

The heat rose in Claire's face. Her chest tightened, and she wished she could take the words back. The comment itself was brief, but what it activated in her was not. Claire had built her career on bringing fresh ideas, on being the person who could see around corners. Being dismissed so quickly did not just sting; it cut into her sense of identity. The story in her head shifted instantly: Maybe I do not belong here.

As the conversation moved forward, she began noticing things she had not seen at first. Raj leaned forward as if ready to speak, then hesitated when Marco's expression hardened. He cleared his throat and let the thought go. Jason, usually animated, dropped his gaze to his notebook and began scribbling without purpose, his shoulders sinking. The air in the room grew heavier.

To an outsider, the meeting still looked efficient. Slides advanced, deadlines were noted, and Marco moved briskly from point to point. But beneath the surface, the team had gone quiet. Voices that had been ready to contribute minutes earlier had withdrawn. People were protecting themselves, choosing silence over risk.

For Claire, it was the moment the warnings from lunch crystallized. What she felt in her own chest, the sudden doubt and the urge to shrink back, was mirrored across the table. The trigger was not hers alone. It belonged to the group. Marco's dismissal had signaled, as it always did, that certain contributions were not safe. And with that signal, the team shifted from open engagement to guarded self-protection. That is the power of a trigger. It does not just tug on surface emotions; it presses on the parts of us that are wired to seek belonging, influence, or control. This is why the reaction often feels outsized. We are not simply responding to what happened; we are responding to what our mind decided it meant.

And when a trigger fires, it usually lights up one or more points on your Behavior Compass:

- **North – Values.** If collaboration is one of your core values, being left out of a decision might feel like a personal attack.
- **East – Beliefs.** If you hold the belief that good leaders are always in control, any moment of uncertainty might ignite shame.
- **South – Thoughts.** If your inner script whispers "You are never enough," even mild feedback can set it off.

- **West – Emotions.** If frustration is already simmering, a minor inconvenience can send it spilling over.

The compass itself is not the problem. It is the signal. The question is whether you recognize it as a cue to pay attention, or whether you let it sweep you into autopilot.

When Triggers Become False Comfort

Not every trigger feels painful. Some feel like validation. That is the tricky part. When you get praise that reinforces a belief such as "I am only valuable if I work later than everyone else," the trigger feels good in the moment. It comes with a rush of affirmation, the satisfaction of being noticed, the sense that the sacrifice was worth it. The same is true when a team member is constantly recognized for sending emails late at night. "Why are you working so late?" becomes recognition. On the surface, it looks like commitment, but underneath it quietly teaches everyone that visibility comes from exhaustion, not from impact. These moments of recognition are powerful, but they can also be dangerous, because they reward habits that may look impressive while quietly eroding balance, trust, and long-term effectiveness. It is the same when someone confirms your frustration about another department. On the surface, it feels like alignment. You are not alone; someone else sees what you see. The agreement creates a moment of relief, a quick bond. But beneath the surface, it deepens the divide. Instead of moving toward solutions, the team slips into complaint cycles that sound collaborative but are actually corrosive. And here is where the brain wiring we explored earlier comes back into play. When our minds recognize a pattern, even a negative one, it becomes easier to continue the narrative than to disrupt it. Familiarity feels safer than uncertainty. So the story gets told again and again, and each retelling makes the frustration feel truer, more justified, and harder to challenge. What begins as a moment of shared validation becomes a loop of reinforcement that narrows perspective and makes forward momentum almost impossible.

That is the danger of false comfort. It masquerades as connection, but it is really inertia. It gives you the illusion of being anchored, when in reality you are tied to something that is holding you back.

Claire saw this in the weeks after her first meeting with Marco. At lunch one afternoon, Jason leaned across the table and said quietly, "You handled yourself fine in there. Honestly, most of us don't even bother speaking up anymore. It's not worth the energy." His tone was supportive, even protective. Claire nodded, grateful for the reassurance, but something about it unsettled her.

What felt like solidarity was also resignation. Jason's words confirmed her own hesitation, making it easier to pull back rather than try again. She realized later that she had confused validation with safety. What looked like encouragement was actually an invitation to lower her voice and accept the culture as it was. It felt good in the moment, but it was keeping her small.

False comfort shows up across the Behavior Compass:

- **Values.** A leader who prizes reliability is praised for never taking time off. The recognition feels aligned, but the hidden story is that rest is weakness.
- **Beliefs.** A manager believes good leaders always have answers. When colleagues thank her for her decisiveness, the praise cements the belief, even when it would be wiser to pause and ask questions.
- **Thoughts.** An employee carries the script "I am only useful if I do more than everyone else." When rewarded for going above and beyond, the thought is confirmed, but the habit becomes unsustainable.
- **Emotions.** A team vents together about how hard change is. The shared frustration bonds them, but the emotional loop keeps them circling the problem rather than moving forward.

In each case, the trigger does not feel like a threat. It feels like a compliment, a moment of recognition, or the relief of being understood. Yet it quietly reinforces patterns that are limiting.

This is why noticing your triggers matters. They are not only red flags for pain, they are also yellow lights for comfort zones that masquerade as alignment. A yellow light is not a reason to slam on the brakes, but it is a cue to pay attention. It signals that what feels familiar may not be what moves you forward.

The brain is wired for shortcuts. It loves confirmation, whether positive or negative, because confirmation requires less energy than reconsidering. This is why false comfort is so sticky. It rewards the path you are already on, even if that path is narrowing.

Leaders who ignore false comfort end up mistaking activity for progress, consensus for alignment, and praise for growth. Leaders who notice false comfort learn to ask the harder question: Does this recognition, this agreement, or this validation expand what is possible, or does it shrink it?

The Group Effect

Triggers do not live in individuals alone. They ripple across teams. One person shuts down in a meeting, and the silence becomes contagious. A leader's frustration shows up in clipped replies, and suddenly everyone else is walking on eggshells. Triggers multiply because teams are emotional systems. When one person is activated, the group feels it. That is exactly what Claire experienced. Her moment of dismissal was not isolated. Raj, Jason, and others mirrored it in their own ways, creating a ripple effect that reinforced the very culture her teammates had warned her about at lunch. What began as one sharp comment turned into a collective withdrawal, an unspoken agreement that the safest path was silence.

The Reframe

The purpose of understanding triggers is not to eliminate them. That is impossible. The purpose is to use them as mirrors. Every trigger holds up a reflection of what you value, believe, think, or feel. It is less about the spark itself and more about the story beneath it.

So when you feel that sudden rush of heat in your chest, or the quiet withdrawal into yourself, pause and ask: *What did this moment just light up in me? Was it a value being pressed? A belief being challenged? A thought on repeat? An emotion I did not expect?* That reflection is where the power lies. Because once you can name it, you can choose how to respond. Without that pause, the trigger runs you. With it, the trigger informs you.

North – Values: When They're Challenged (or Over-Confirmed)

When a trigger hits your values, it's not subtle. You feel it. Deep in your gut, sometimes before your brain catches up. Imagine you're having a tough conversation, and the other person questions your integrity and says to you, "I think you're lying". If integrity is one of your core values, you're not just processing words; you're feeling attacked at your foundation. Your jaw tightens. Your chest heats up. The urge to defend, shut down, or walk out doesn't come from nowhere; it comes from something sacred being hit. Values aren't preferences. They're your non-negotiables. When they're challenged, your body reacts faster than your logic can catch up.

But values don't only show up in conflict. Sometimes they slip into the driver's seat in ways that quietly steer you off course. A value, when over-confirmed, can start to masquerade as identity. The pursuit of excellence can harden into perfectionism. A commitment to loyalty can become blind allegiance. A value like harmony, when left unchecked, can turn into avoidance of healthy debate. In these moments, what once steadied you begins to narrow your options instead of expanding them.

This is why it's worth pausing to check the calibration. A value should act like a compass needle, pointing you toward what matters most, not like a weight that keeps you from moving. Ask yourself:

- *What value feels most activated in this moment?*
- *Is it helping me evolve, or is it quietly keeping me in place?*
- *If I loosened my grip on this value just slightly, what new perspective might I see?*

The goal isn't to discard what matters. It's to notice when your values are functioning as anchors and when they've slipped into anchor chains. That awareness alone can change how you interpret the signal and how you choose to respond.

East – Beliefs: When They're Shaken (or Reinforced Too Strongly)

Beliefs are the lens you use to interpret what's happening around you. But here's the thing, just because you believe something doesn't make it true. Most beliefs aren't facts. They're filters. Built from years of experience, both good and bad. Formed in moments of trust and moments of letdown. A belief may come from a boss who once dismissed your ideas… or from a team culture in which only the loudest voices got heard. And when a trigger taps into one of those old beliefs? Your brain doesn't ask, *"Is this still accurate?"* It just says, *"Yep, this again."*

Maybe your belief is, *"Leaders say they want feedback, but they don't mean it."* So, when your comment gets brushed off in a meeting, it doesn't feel like a one-time moment; it feels like proof of that belief. Or maybe you believe, *"I have to handle everything myself or it won't get done right."* Then, when someone offers to help, it doesn't feel like support; it feels like a threat to your value.

But here's the twist: it's not just negative beliefs that hold us back. Sometimes we're most stuck when we're reinforcing beliefs that feel good. If you believe *"I'm the fixer,"* or *"I'm the one everyone relies on,"* that belief might be fueling your overwork, your burnout, or even your resentment. Because you're no longer showing up from purpose, you're showing up to protect a belief that may not be serving you anymore. Here's the reflection:

- *Where did this belief come from, and does it still serve me?*
- *Is this belief moving me forward, or is it keeping me in place?*
- *If I released or reframed this belief, what new possibility might open up?*

South – Thoughts: When They Spiral (or Sound Too Familiar)

Thoughts are the quiet scripts running behind the scenes. They don't shout. They just loop. Over and over. And the more often you think a thought, the truer it *feels*, whether it is or not.

You might recognize the spirals: *"This is my fault." "I should've seen this coming." "If I don't get this right, I'll lose credibility."* Sometimes the spiral is fast and obvious. But more often? It's subtle and practiced. It's the familiar script you've run so many times you don't even notice it anymore.

But thoughts don't have to be negative to throw you off. Sometimes the thoughts that keep us stuck are the ones that sound like competence or responsibility.

- *"I'll just handle it myself."*

- *"I know what needs to be done and I don't have time to explain it."*
- *"Everyone on the team is completely overwhelmed, so I have to do it."*

Sound productive? Sure. But those thoughts are often driven by over-functioning, anxiety, or an outdated belief about your role. And the more they repeat, the more they crowd out possibility. That's how we trade intentional leadership for autopilot.

The question isn't *"Are my thoughts positive?"* The better question is: *"Are my thoughts aligned with who I want to be in this moment, or are they just the fastest route to feeling in control?"*

West – Emotions: When They Hijack (or Quietly Dictate)

Emotions don't wait for an invitation. They show up, whether we want them to or not. And in high-change environments, they're usually first in the room. Frustration. Fear. Shame. Resentment. Sometimes they're loud. Sometimes they're buried so deep, they come out sideways, in sarcasm, silence, over-apologizing, or that weird tension you can't quite name but *everyone* can feel.

Most organizations teach people how to manage emotions by hiding them. "Be professional." "Don't take it personally." "Keep it together." The problem? That doesn't make the emotion go away. It just forces it underground until it erupts in ways no one sees coming.

And then there's the flip side, the moments when we're so emotionally aligned with a situation that we don't *want* to question it. We stay in what feels emotionally safe: the trusted team member we've always defended; the system we helped build; the story we've always told ourselves. But just because an emotion feels familiar doesn't mean it's helping you lead. Comfort and clarity are not the same thing.

This is why emotional self-awareness isn't soft. It's strategic. Because when you know what you're feeling, and why, you're far less likely to let that emotion drive decisions you'll later regret.

Emotions don't always speak in capital letters. More often, they whisper through behavior, tone, or the phrases we've all learned to say when we're trying to stay composed. But underneath? There's usually something else going on.

Here are a few examples of how to read between the lines, not to assume, but to *get curious*:

When they say: "I'm fine."
It might mean: "I don't feel safe enough to speak up."
When they say: "It's no big deal."
It might mean: "I don't think you'll take it seriously if I say what I'm really feeling."

When they say: "I'm just tired."
It might mean: "I'm emotionally exhausted, and I don't have the words for it."
When they say: "Sure, whatever you think is best."
It might mean: "I've stopped believing my voice matters here."
When they say: "We've already tried that."
It might mean: "I'm still carrying disappointment from last time."
When they say: "This is just how we do it."
It might mean: "I'm afraid of what will happen if we change."
When they say: "I didn't think it was important to bring up."
It might mean: "I've learned that naming hard things comes with consequences."
When they say: "It's all good."
It might mean: "I don't trust this space enough to be honest."
When they say: "I'm over it."
It might mean: "I'm not over it, I'm just done trying to talk about it."
When they say nothing at all?
It might mean: "This culture has taught me silence is safer than honesty."

These are not one-size-fits-all translations. But they are cues, moments to pause and ask, "What's underneath that response?" Because the best leaders don't react to the words alone. They respond to the story the words are protecting. So ask yourself: *What's the emotion behind the reaction? And is it asking for attention, or control?*

When your Behavior Compass gets activated, whether it's through misalignment or over-comfort, it's sending you a signal. The values that feel violated. The beliefs that feel threatened. The thoughts that start spinning. The emotions that take over the room, even if no one says a word. The point isn't to shut it down. The point is to pay attention. Because behavior doesn't just "happen." It's driven by what's underneath. And the more you understand the signal, the more clearly you can choose your next move. That's where self-awareness becomes leadership.

To help you practice, you'll find a Trigger Reflection Worksheet in the back of this book, or you can download a printable version anytime at ThEevolutionaryMindset.com/Tools.

Part III

Leading the Evolution

Chapter 8

Reaction vs. Response

Let's start with a simple truth: Reactivity is fast. It's familiar. And for most of us, it's the default setting. You don't have to think about it. You just... do it. Your jaw tightens. Your tone sharpens. You hit send before your better judgment has even had a chance to enter the room. And if we're being honest, we've all been *that person*, the one who hits "Reply All" to an email that really should have been a sidebar conversation... with a different tone, a lower heart rate, and maybe a little less sarcasm.

That's reactivity in action. It's not a character flaw, it's wiring. As we explored back in Chapter 2, your brain isn't built for nuance under pressure. It's built for speed. When it detects a threat, whether it's a missed deadline, a challenging comment, or someone sighing too loudly in a high-stakes meeting, it jumps into action. Fight. Flight. Freeze. Forward snarky email. It doesn't ask what's *useful*, it asks what's *fast*. And while that impulse might have helped our ancestors avoid being eaten by tigers, it's a little less helpful in a team meeting where someone just questioned your strategy.

Reactivity gives us the illusion of control. But more often than not, it's just your nervous system hijacking the mic and saying, "Don't worry, I've got this", when in reality, it absolutely does *not* have this. If you've ever said something sharp in a meeting and immediately regretted it, or hit send and then stared at your screen like, "Well, that escalated quickly," you're not alone. You're just human. And human brains under stress tend to move faster than our leadership wants them to. The good news? That reaction doesn't have to be the end of the story. But to shift it, we have to understand what's happening in that moment, and what it's costing us. Reactivity tricks us. It gives the illusion of momentum. You respond fast, speak with conviction, take charge of the room, and for a split second, it feels like leadership. Like action. Like control. But more often than not, what it actually creates is confusion, defensiveness, or a team that leaves the meeting wondering what just happened and who's going to clean it up.

This is one of the biggest traps in high-change environments. When everything feels urgent, reactivity can feel like clarity. But speed isn't the same thing as strategy, and volume isn't the same thing as influence. Slamming your laptop shut or rattling off a directive might make you feel like you've "handled it," but all you've really done is pass your discomfort downstream. And now your team is spending the next three days decoding your tone, avoiding your calendar invites, or venting in Slack DMs titled "ugh."

I once worked for a senior leader who was smart, high-performing, and completely unpredictable. You never knew which version of him you were going to get, but you did know that a 1:1 meeting at 4 p.m. was a bad idea. Late afternoon seemed to be the danger zone. By then, the caffeine had worn off, the patience had thinned out, and the likelihood of being in someone's crosshairs had tripled. He wasn't cruel, he was reactive. He let his emotional residue from the day lead the conversation, and eventually, people started walking on eggshells and stopped bringing anything real to the table. Not because they didn't care, but because they didn't want to be collateral damage.

That's what reactivity does. It might feel good in the moment, a quick release, a show of force, but it costs you on the back end. Trust erodes. Communication gets distorted. And instead of forward momentum, you end up with teams who are busy managing your moods instead of managing the mission.

This doesn't mean you have to tiptoe around every tough conversation or become the office emotional support animal. But if your reaction feels disproportionately satisfying? It probably wasn't strategic. It was survival. And survival isn't leadership. Not long-term. Not where it counts.

The Intention Gap

There's a space, often only a few seconds long, between the moment something activates you and the moment you act on it. It's the space between what you feel and what you choose. And while it might sound small, that space holds more power than most people realize. It's where your leadership either defaults to reaction or rises into response. I call it the Intention Gap.

The Intention Gap isn't passive. It's not avoidance, hesitation, or overthinking. It's the most active form of leadership you can practice. Because what happens inside that pause, between stimulus and response, is what defines how you show up. It's the internal checkpoint where your wiring meets your wisdom. Where you stop long enough to ask, Is this emotion trying to protect me, or does this moment need something else from me?

If Chapter 2 offered anything, it's that the brain is built for speed, not nuance. It's wired to protect, not to pause. When something triggers discomfort, an email that feels off, a tone that cuts sharper than expected, a decision that catches you off guard, your system races to react. And if you haven't built the habit of slowing that reaction down, the impulse wins. Not because you're a bad leader, but because your nervous system got there first.

Nora is a perfect example. For years, she powered through pushback with logic and slides. Quick, sharp reactions that felt efficient to her but slowly cost her team their trust. They stopped offering dissent, not because they agreed, but because they did not want to be on the receiving end of her tone. What Nora didn't realize at the time was that every reaction was teaching her team something: stay quiet, keep your head down, avoid the risk of speaking up. It took one pivotal meeting for her to see that her presence, not her presentation, was shaping the room.

That meeting took place on a Wednesday afternoon, the kind of meeting everyone dreads. The strategy team had been running hot for weeks, and the launch deadline loomed like a storm cloud over everything. By the time Nora walked into the room, the tension was visible. Laptops were open, but no one was typing. Coffee cups sat untouched. A couple of people exchanged glances that said more than words ever could.

Nora set her bag down and opened her slides. She had rehearsed her points and had a plan for steering the conversation back to focus. Still, she felt it in the room, resistance humming just under the surface.

Ten minutes in, Sam, one of her managers, cleared his throat. He was thoughtful by nature, rarely one to stir the pot. Which made his words all the heavier. "I need to raise a concern about the launch date."

Nora's jaw tightened. Her heart kicked faster. She knew where this was going. The words loaded in her mind, sharp and ready: *We do not have time to revisit this.*

But then she remembered. The last few months had taught her that every reaction had a cost. And in that split second, she chose something different.

She leaned back in her chair and deliberately unclenched her fists. "Give me a second," she said, steadying her voice. The room went quiet, all eyes turning toward her.

"Okay," she continued, looking straight at Sam. "Help me understand what is underneath the concern."

Sam hesitated. He glanced around the table, as if to check if anyone would back him up. Finally, he exhaled. "I am worried we're optimizing for speed and not for sustainability. If we launch like this, my team will burn out in the first month."

In the past, Nora might have cut him off, countered with logic, or reminded him of the stakes. Instead, she paused. She nodded. "That is fair," she said. "Let's map what is non-negotiable for the timeline and where we actually have room. I do not want us winning the quarter and losing the year."

Across the table, Priya, another manager, spoke up. She had been sitting with arms crossed, but now she leaned in. "If we protect the customer promise and shift two technicians for forty-eight hours, we can absorb the risk."

"Good," Nora said, her tone steady but collaborative. "Then name the smallest slice we can ship without breaking trust, and write the sentence we will tell customers. No hedging."

The dam broke. One by one, people began to contribute. A junior analyst, who had been silent the entire meeting, finally offered, "If we reframe the customer update this way, it will land better." Another added, "We could reroute two of the downstream tasks without pulling the whole schedule apart." The energy shifted. What had started as tension began to feel like problem-solving. Pens scratched across notepads. People leaned forward instead of away. Even the skeptics, the ones who had been privately venting in the hallways, found their voices. The decision they came to still carried trade-offs. It was not painless. But it was trusted.

When the meeting ended, Nora sat back in her chair. For the first time in weeks, she could feel the room settle instead of splinter. She realized that the real turning point had not been in the slides she prepared or the arguments she rehearsed. It had been in the pause she bought, the presence she chose, and the question she asked. That single beat shifted the trajectory of trust.

That is the Intention Gap in action. It does not erase discomfort, but it changes what happens inside of it. Nora's pause shifted her from instinct to influence. Instead of letting her nervous system take over the meeting, she chose presence, and in doing so, she changed the trajectory of the conversation.

This is the power of the gap. Sometimes it is nothing more than a breath, a clarifying question, or a posture shift. Yet inside that pause is the chance to move from autopilot to agency. Leaders who can consistently step into that space are not only regulating themselves, they are actively reshaping the culture around them.

And like any bridge, the Intention Gap needs structure. That structure is everything we have been building throughout the chapters leading up to this one. Emotional stamina gives you the strength to stay present. Awareness of your triggers shows you what is being activated. The Behavior Compass reveals whether it is a value, belief, thought, or emotion pulling the strings. Together, they prepare you for the gap. The Compass tells you what is alive; the Gap gives you the space to decide what to do with it.

In high-stakes environments, that pause becomes the place where trust is built, where psychological safety begins, and where the Evolutionary Mindset stops being an idea and becomes culture.

It is the difference between a leader who explodes in a meeting and one who says, "Something is off here, let me take a moment." The first reaction might feel powerful in the moment, but the second builds power over time. The leaders who earn lasting influence are not the ones with the quickest answers. They are the ones who have trained themselves to pause, to take a breath, to check their Compass, to cross the Intention Gap before speaking from a place they cannot walk back.

It is not about being slow. It is about being sure. And in high-stakes environments, that pause is where trust is built, where psychological safety begins, and where the Evolutionary Mindset moves from theory to practice.

You do not build the Intention Gap in theory; you build it in practice. In real conversations, with real stakes, and with real people watching how you handle pressure. It is easy to talk about pause and presence when everything is calm. The real test is when the room is tense, the deadline is closing in, or someone challenges you in front of your team. In those moments, the gap either holds or collapses, and what happens in that space carries weight. You are either modeling steadiness or volatility. Teams do not just hear your words; they mirror your pace, your tone, and your presence. The gap is where psychological safety is reinforced or eroded, where trust compounds or leaks, and where direction becomes clearer or more confusing. And steadiness is not something you can will yourself into, it is something you train.

So, how do you build the ability to respond instead of react? Not in theory, but right in the middle of the meeting, the conversation, the tension? You don't need a 90-day habit tracker. What you need are micro-practices. Simple, repeatable moves that strengthen your ability to pause, re-center, and choose what comes next. Think of them as quick resets you can return to in real time, when the room heats up and your logic starts to slip.

Here are six I've taught, used, and watched transform how leaders show up under pressure.

1. Name the Signal

Notice when your system is getting activated. For me, it's a tight jaw or spike in urgency. For others, it might be racing thoughts or the urge to interrupt. When that shows up, don't push through it. Just name it. "I'm activated. This moment matters." That's the cue to pause instead of powering forward.

2. Buy a Beat

Literally, pause. Take one breath. Sip your water. Say something like, "Let me think about that for a second," or "I want to make sure I'm answering this clearly." These aren't stall tactics. They're deliberate choices that give your logic time to catch up with your emotion.

3. Check the Compass

Use the Behavior Compass as a quick gut check: What value just got hit? What belief flared up?

What thought is spinning? What emotion is tugging at you? You don't have to fix it in the moment; just naming it breaks the autopilot. (If you need a refresher, flip back to Chapter 3 or grab the download below.)

4. **Reset your Body**

Your nervous system listens to your posture more than your thoughts. Drop your shoulders. Unclench your jaw. Plant your feet. Sit back or stand tall. Signal to your system: "I am safe. I am steady. I am still leading."

5. **Use an Anchor Phrase**

Keep a stick note on your laptop, your planner, or wherever you tend to get activated. It could say: "Respond, don't react." Or "Pause to lead." Or even "Hold space, not control." Words only work if they're repeated. Make it a habit, not a gimmick.

6. **Call in a Signal Buddy**

Sometimes you're too in it to notice. That's when you need someone in the room who can give you the "nose swipe" or send a "slow down" or "pause" message in chat. Agree on the signal ahead of time. Tell them what your tells are. Let them help you catch yourself before the reactivity wins.

Over time, these practices create muscle memory. You start to notice the moments that used to hijack you. You start to shift your language mid-sentence. You begin to *feel* the gap open, and step into it with more confidence. And that's where your influence grows. Not because you always have the perfect answer, but because you're leading from a place your team can trust.

Mirror Moment

What conversation, if slowed by one breath, might have gone differently,

and what would it take to lead from response instead of reaction next time?

The moment you start practicing response over reaction, people notice. Not because you make a big announcement or roll out a new team charter, but because your presence shifts. You listen differently. You pause when things get tense. You choose words that de-escalate instead of dominate. And that presence? It's contagious.

Teams mirror what they're led through. If you model reactivity, they'll start playing defense. If you model response, they'll start practicing it, too, often without even realizing it. That's the quiet power of culture. It doesn't need a policy to exist. It just needs a pattern.

And here's the good news: you don't have to turn your team into a mindfulness circle or start every meeting with deep breathing (unless you want to). You just need to give people permission to pause. To say, "Let's take a breath before we respond to that." Or "What's the most helpful response here, not the fastest one?" Small phrases, modeled consistently, become signals that this is a team that doesn't just default to noise; we choose clarity.

You can even name the Intention Gap with your team. Not in a "let me teach you a concept from my leadership book" kind of way, but in a human, grounded way. Try something like, "I've noticed I tend to jump in too quickly when I feel challenged. I'm working on slowing down my response, especially in high-stakes moments. If you see me getting reactive, feel free to call me back to the moment. I'll do the same for you if I see it." I worked with one team that used the word "bananas" to call out the discomfort in the room. It was a funny word that broke the tension without putting someone on edge. That kind of leadership doesn't weaken your authority; it strengthens your credibility.

Because what you're doing in that moment is modeling *self-regulation in real time*. And that, more than any agenda or strategy deck, is what creates safety. When people know they won't be steamrolled for speaking up or ambushed for getting it wrong, they fully bring their minds and voices to the room. And that's when momentum starts.

Let's be honest, reactivity isn't going away. It'll still show up when you're tired, when things feel personal, or when change arrives faster than your brain can process it. The goal isn't to eliminate reactivity altogether. It's to recognize it sooner and recover faster. To stretch the space between emotion and action just long enough to choose the version of yourself that leads forward, not loops backward.

So, here's your reflection:

Where in your leadership do you feel most reactive? Is it when you feel challenged? When decisions are made without you? When timelines shift?

Identify the pattern (trigger) and start building the pause.

What signal does your body send when you're about to react? And what micro-practice can you start using to slow it down, even just once this week?

What phrase or word can your team rally around to call out when the moments are escalating and need to be grounded?

And finally, who's your person? The one who can give you the signal when you're too in it to notice? Find them. Tell them. Let them help you.

Because this isn't about being perfect. It's about being intentional. And leadership, at its core, is a series of high-stakes moments where your response matters more than your plan. You don't need to know everything. You just need to own the space between stimulus and response, and use it to build trust, one choice at a time.

Chapter 9

Consistency, Not Intensity

Real evolution doesn't come from intensity. It comes from consistency. Not from massive action plans or sweeping declarations, but from small, deliberate moves practiced over time. The Evolutionary Mindset recognizes that sustainable change happens one intentional choice at a time. It's not about launching a dozen initiatives on Monday and hoping something sticks. It's about picking one thing, one behavior, one question, one lens, and committing to practicing it until it becomes a natural part of how you lead and how your team operates. The goal isn't to build a sudden surge of energy; it's to build a steady rhythm that people can recognize, trust, and lean into when everything else feels uncertain.

Consistency beats intensity because it scales. It builds trust in the middle of transition and creates stability when the path ahead feels unpredictable. When leaders pick one part of the work to approach differently and practice it consistently, they show their teams that the change isn't performative, it's foundational. It's not just a flash of new energy; it's a new way of thinking, one that isn't dependent on adrenaline or urgency. And that steady presence, even when it feels ordinary, builds more true momentum over time than any single burst of urgency ever could. Real leadership isn't about the energy you can generate on launch day; it's about the resilience you build every day after that.

This is why choosing where to start matters. You don't have to tackle everything at once, and you shouldn't try. Maybe you start by consistently asking, "For what purpose?" before launching a new project. Maybe you choose to pause and check your Behavior Compass before major decisions, anchoring yourself in how you should respond instead of reacting from urgency. Maybe you begin every Monday meeting with a two-minute check-in, asking, "Looking back at last week, where did we mistake discomfort for danger?" It's not about doing it all or perfecting it immediately. It's about doing one thing with clear intention and doing it often enough that it becomes part of the team's natural reflex, not something special, but something expected.

Leaders often underestimate how much credibility is built through small, repeated moves. Trust doesn't come from grand speeches or glossy mission statements; it comes from seeing leadership show up the same way on the good days and the hard days. It grows when a team knows that the focus they hear about today will still be the focus a month from now, and that the leadership promises made aren't just another round of performative change management. Consistency brings clarity and focus, which naturally reduces both change fatigue and resistance. When teams experience that kind of steady leadership, they stop bracing for change as a storm to survive and start evolving with it. They begin to look forward to the continual evolution of necessary changes that drive the business forward, changes they get to be part of, not victims of. They can see and feel the steady hand of leadership guiding the way, asking better questions, and providing transparency even when the answers aren't perfect. Over time, they stop wondering whether leadership is serious about change and start believing it, because they see it lived out consistently, not just preached when it's convenient. Consistency sends a message louder than any all-hands meeting or rollout campaign ever could: this matters enough to practice, it matters enough to be patient, and it matters enough to stay with it even when the excitement wears off. When teams see that modeled, they start mirroring it, too.

One of the most powerful practices I have seen a team put into place came from an unexpected challenge. I was leading a team that supported an organization in a near-constant state of change. Every other month brought a new shift. Some were uncomfortable. Others were deeply challenging. And if you let it, your thoughts could easily pull you down the rabbit hole of worry, cynicism, and negativity. To combat that, we started a simple but powerful practice: for every difficult situation we faced, we identified three positives. I didn't brush off their frustration or minimize their emotions; I created space for what they needed to say, to process, and to grieve if necessary. But after that, we shifted the focus and worked together, compassionately, to identify what good could come from the change. Sometimes the answers were broad-reaching, touching many layers of the business. Other times, they were deeply personal. The positives varied as much as the initiatives did, but the habit remained the same. Over time, this practice rewired how the team approached uncertainty. They learned to seek what they wanted to find. They wanted to find fulfillment. They wanted to see their impact. They wanted to believe they were making a difference, not just surviving change, but actively shaping it. And because they looked for it, they found it. After all, you will always find what you are looking for.

Mirror Moment

What's one small move you could practice this week, not for impact, but for rhythm?

Evolution doesn't ask for perfection or intensity. It asks for intention. It asks for leaders who are willing to start with one small move and stay with it, not until it's exciting, but until it's expected. Until it's part of how decisions are made, how meetings are run, and how people show up for each other. You don't need a calendar full of new commitments. Just one. One that you revisit, practice, and model until it becomes muscle memory. Because culture isn't built in bursts, it's built in the moments that repeat.

In the next chapter, I am going to share one of the ways you can consistently practice an Evolutionary Mindset with the Compass Check-in.

Chapter 10

Presence Over Pressure

The first time I led our senior leadership team meeting, I was laser-focused on one thing: don't screw it up.

The conference room itself didn't help. It was one of those executive spaces designed to impress, with a wall of glass windows that opened to a sweeping view of the Colorado Front Range. On clear days, the mountains stood so close you could see the snow ridges carved into their peaks. On hazy ones, the light streamed in thick and golden, bouncing off the table until everyone had to squint against the glare. It was the kind of view that made you want to pause, take it in, and maybe even feel a little small in the best way. But pausing wasn't on my agenda that morning.

I had the agenda lined up, timed down to the minute. My leader had given me a pre-meeting pep talk that could be summed up in three words: *Stay. On. Track.* Translation? Don't let anyone hijack the room. Efficiency was the goal. This group didn't tolerate drift. If the meeting lost steam or went sideways, they'd check out fast. Even worse, I'd seen some of them use the slightest detour to grab airtime, a quick derail disguised as "thought partnership," but really just a stage to perform on. I knew exactly who he was talking about. My job was to keep us moving.

The truth is, I was still new in this role, still finding my footing. On paper, I had already earned the seat. But in my head, I was proving, maybe more to myself than to anyone else, that I belonged there. So, I gripped the agenda a little tighter. I clicked through the slides a little cleaner. And for the first thirty minutes, it felt like it was working. The room was following along, and no one had gone off course.

Until the room shifted.

I walked the group through the plan for our upcoming succession planning sessions, who would be included, how we'd prepare, and what would be expected from each of them. The slides were straightforward, no fluff, just the framework we'd agreed on. I kept my delivery steady, moving point by point, watching the clock to make sure we stayed on schedule. For the first half hour, everything felt controlled. The group followed along, a few heads nodding here and there, no side debates pulling us off track.

Then Shira leaned in.

She had a way of doing it that always changed the room. "Before we finalize these sessions," she said, her tone sharper than the words themselves, "we need to decide how honest we're really going to be with managers. Are these conversations about development, or are we actually prepared to talk about readiness? Because those are two very different things."

The question hung in the air. She wasn't wrong. It was a good point. But the way she said it, cutting in just as we were settling into a rhythm, made my pulse spike. My leader's voice came back, clear as if he were sitting at the table: *Stay. On. Track.*

Shira didn't push back in her chair. She leaned in further, looking straight at me. "If we wait until the prep sessions to figure this out, we'll already be behind. These conversations can go sideways fast, and managers are going to feel the inconsistency. We should be talking about this now, not later."

Her words weren't reckless; they were strategic. She wanted airtime, and she knew exactly how to get it. A few heads around the table turned her way, waiting to see how I'd respond.

I felt the heat rise in my chest. I had two options: let the conversation detour into the weeds, or pull us back. And I already knew what my leader would expect. *Stay. On. Track.* So, I kept my voice even, but firm. "That's a fair concern, Shira, and I agree consistency matters. But the design of the sessions accounts for that. We'll address those issues together in detail. Right now, we need to confirm the timing, so everything stays on track."

The words were professional. Polite. But final.

Shira's expression didn't soften. If anything, the edge in her eyes sharpened, as if she was making a note, not just about the topic, but about me.

Across the table, Michelle kept her pen in hand, but she stopped writing. She had that calm presence that rarely wavered, but in moments like this, her silence was its own signal. She didn't interrupt, didn't weigh in, but the pause told me she was processing more than I'd given space for. If she had concerns, she wasn't about to fight for airtime against Shira. She'd hold it, and maybe bring it up later, but it was hanging there, unspoken.

June, seated a few chairs down, looked between us. She didn't rush in either, but her face carried the kind of quiet empathy that made people trust her. She had a gift for softening hard edges, for pulling threads together when conversations threatened to unravel. And for a moment, I could see she was debating whether to step into the gap. Her pen hovered just above her page, her eyes flicking from Shira to me, weighing if this was the moment to bridge.

But before she could speak, Travis jumped in.

"Look," he said, his loud voice cutting across the tension, "this isn't about prep. We've had the same names sitting on these lists for years, tagged for multiple roles, and when the positions actually open up, they're never the ones selected. We're not having enough real conversations about that. And frankly, we're doing a disservice, because people start to believe they're next in line when they're not. The real problem is the pipeline itself. Half the names on those lists aren't realistic. We can polish the process all we want, but pretending the pipeline is solid doesn't make it true."

The words landed hard. Not shouted. Not dramatic. Just direct enough that no one could ignore them.

For a moment, no one spoke. The kind of pause that stretched longer than it should have. Shira glanced back at me, a flicker of triumph in her eyes as if to say, *See? I'm not the only one pushing this.* Michelle leaned back slightly in her chair, lips pressed tight, her silence confirming that Travis had voiced what others were already thinking. June lowered her eyes to her notes, pen resting against the page but unmoving, her stillness almost louder than words.

The room, which just minutes before had been orderly and efficient, was suddenly heavy. The truth was out. It was raw, uncomfortable, and hanging in the air like a live wire. All it needed was someone to pick it up.

And in that moment, all eyes turned to me.

I could feel the weight of the room pressing in, every eye waiting to see what I would do with Travis's comment. For a split second, I thought about leaning into it, letting the conversation open up. But just as quickly, my leader's prep talk echoed back in my mind. *Stay. On. Track. Keep the agenda moving.*

So, I did exactly that.

I forced my tone even and said, "Like I said, we'll capture those concerns in the sessions themselves. We haven't built in time for those discussions today. For now, let's stick with the agenda." And I clicked to the next slide.

It was the professional answer. The controlled answer. And the wrong answer. And it went over like a diaper in a hot car. The energy drained out of the room almost instantly. June gazed over at me and held eye contact just long enough for me to know I'd made the wrong move. Michelle didn't say a word; she just wrote slowly, as if she were recording the moment rather than contributing to it. Shira sat back, arms crossed, her point made whether or not I'd acknowledged it. And Travis, bold, loud Travis, went quiet, leaning into his chair with a look that said he was done for now.

I had kept us "on track," but I'd lost the room.

Later that afternoon, I sat at my desk trying to bury myself in emails. It was the kind of mindless busy work that made me feel productive without requiring me to think too much, exactly what I wanted after the morning's meeting. My inbox was overflowing, and I was clicking through it with a kind of desperate focus, my mind constantly replaying the session and "should-of'ing" all over myself.

That's when the door slid open. No knock. No pause. Just the sharp shift of the glass door against the frame that made me look up. I hadn't invited anyone in, which is why I felt that jolt of surprise when Michelle stepped through. I didn't feel like talking to anyone.

She didn't ask permission. She didn't even slow down. She crossed the room with her usual steadiness and lowered herself into the chair across from me as if it were already hers.

She didn't fidget, didn't look around, didn't soften the entry with small talk. She simply sat, crossed one leg over the other, leaned back, and let the silence hang long enough for me to realize she had come with something to say.

Finally, she spoke. "You know you're going to have to recover from that, right?"

Her words caught me off guard. "Recover?" I repeated, though I already knew what she meant.

She nodded, her voice calm but firm. "From shutting it down. You can't just move past comments like that and think people will let it go. They won't. And the next time someone has something important to say, they won't bring it to you. They'll find someone else who will listen. And when that happens, you're not leading the conversation anymore, you're on the outside of it."

I opened my mouth, half-ready to explain that I was doing exactly what I'd been asked to do, that I was following instructions to keep us efficient and on track. But Michelle didn't give me the chance.

"When somebody puts the hard thing on the table," she went on, "that's the moment you have to pay attention to. That's not a distraction. That's the real work. The room was waiting for you to acknowledge it, and you rushed past. You lost them. It happens, but if you don't learn from it, it will keep happening."

She leaned back, her gaze steady but not unkind. "You'll get another chance. But next time, slow down. Give it space. People don't need you to have the perfect answer in the moment. They just need to know you're willing to sit with it."

The office was quiet after she finished, the only sound the faint hum of my computer. I sat back in my chair, her words still echoing. She wasn't dramatic about it, but she was right. I had managed the clock. But I hadn't managed the room. And that difference was everything.

When Michelle finally stood and walked out, she didn't leave with a flourish. No smile. No "good luck." Just the quiet confidence of someone who knew she'd said what needed to be said. The door slid shut behind her, and for the first time all day, the room felt still.

I sat there, staring at my inbox, the cursor blinking in an unfinished draft, but my mind wasn't on emails anymore. Her words lingered, replaying themselves with more clarity than anything I'd heard in that meeting. She was right. I had been so focused on proving I belonged, on running the meeting flawlessly, that I missed the one thing that would have actually shown I belonged: the willingness to pause.

And the truth was, I knew better. I had done better. I'd been in rooms before where I slowed down, asked the harder question, and let the silence fill long enough for people to find their words. I had seen what happened when I leaned into the discomfort instead of pushing past it. But that day, under the weight of a new role and the voice of my leader in my head, I defaulted to control.

That was the day I was reminded that leadership isn't about controlling the dialogue all the time. It's measured by whether people still trust you to hold the real conversation. And once you lose that, you don't just lose momentum. You lose the room.

That's where the Compass Check-In comes in.

You've already been introduced to the Behavior Compass: values, beliefs, thoughts, and emotions. Back in Chapter 3, we used it to map out what might be fueling a behavior after the fact. But in fast-moving rooms, you don't always have time to map. You need to move. And that's what this tool is for.

The Compass Check-In is a real-time pulse check. It's how you spot misalignment before it derails momentum. It's how you course-correct before confusion calcifies into resistance. And it's how you, as a leader, create space in the moment instead of speeding past the signal.

It only takes a minute. But it might change your direction entirely.

So, how do you actually do a Compass Check-In? Don't worry, I didn't just toss you a compass and say, 'Good luck.' I've put together a worksheet that guides you through the process. Try it a few times and soon you'll find yourself doing it without even thinking about it.

You can find the worksheet at the back of this book or at TheEvolutionaryMindset.com/Tools

The Compass Check-In isn't about analyzing or fixing; it's about noticing what's real, naming it, and helping the team move forward with intention. You can run it in your head. You can walk the team through it out loud. You can even write it on a sticky note and keep it next to your screen. It doesn't need to be polished; it just needs to be real.

But here's the thing: This only works if you've done your own work first.

If you haven't taken time to explore your own Compass, your values, your beliefs, your inner narratives, and emotional triggers, this will land flat. The Compass Check-In is a team tool, but it starts with internal alignment. If you skipped Chapter 3 or moved through it quickly, now's the time to revisit it. Because you can't guide a team through misalignment if you're not calibrated yourself.

So, when the room feels off, when engagement dips, or the energy shifts, this is your moment to get R.E.A.L.:

Read the room
Explore what's being protected
Activate the Compass
Lead the shift

Let's break it down:

R – Read the Room

What feels off right now?

Is there tension? Silence? A tone shift? Did someone check out or shut down? You don't need to explain it; you just need to see it. Name what shifted so others don't have to pretend it didn't.

E – Explore What's Being Protected

Is the team guarding status, identity, control, or belonging?

Misalignment is usually a sign that something feels threatened. Maybe someone feels dismissed. Maybe the change is hitting a nerve. Curiosity disarms defensiveness. Ask what might be underneath, not who's "causing the problem."

A – Activate the Compass

Which direction feels fired up, values, beliefs, thoughts, or emotions?

Did a core value get overlooked? Is an old belief quietly running the room? Are thoughts spinning? Are emotions in the driver's seat? You don't need full alignment to move forward, but you do need to see what's in play.

L – Lead the Shift

What's one intentional move we can make together?

It might be pausing the agenda. It might be inviting in a voice that was shut down. It might be acknowledging something that hasn't been said yet. You're not trying to solve the whole problem, just reset the direction.

Let's go back to that meeting and look at how it could have unfolded if I had used R.E.A.L.

You remember the moment. We were halfway through the succession planning agenda when Travis named the thing everyone else had been circling around. The room went quiet. Heads dropped. The energy shifted. And instead of leaning in, I moved us forward. That was the wrong choice.

Here's how it could have sounded if I had paused instead:

Me:

"Before we keep going, I want to pause. We had good energy in this conversation, and then we went silent. That usually means something landed heavier than we've named. Let's stay here for a minute."

The pause would have been uncomfortable. It always is. But silence is often where the real conversation is waiting.

Me again, after a beat:

"I don't think this is just about the prep sessions. It feels deeper, maybe about fairness, expectations, maybe even trust. If that's what's underneath, let's talk about it. This isn't about derailing the plan, it's about making sure the plan is worth following."

And here's what I believe would have happened:

Shira would have leaned in, not to challenge but to confirm. "That's exactly it. If we aren't clear about readiness, managers will handle these conversations differently, and people will hear mixed messages. That hurts credibility."

June would have added her voice, calm but direct. "And it isn't just credibility. It's people's futures. When someone believes they're being groomed for a role they'll never actually get, it can break trust in ways that are hard to repair."

Travis would have doubled down, not to grandstand but to sharpen the truth. "We're not being honest with ourselves about the bench. Half the names on these lists aren't realistic successors. Until we start saying that out loud, we're not solving the problem."

And Michelle, steady, measured Michelle, would have spoken last, pulling the thread tight. "If we want alignment, we can't avoid these conversations. We have to agree on how we'll say the hard thing, not just how we'll run the session."

At this point, I would acknowledge the comments and say, "This is definitely an important conversation, not just for us, but for the employees and the business. We have a few more topics on the agenda, and I don't think we have the time available today to go as deep as this discussion needs to go. And I want to ensure we give them the right amount of space and time. Would you all be okay if we find dedicated time next week before the sessions start for us to discuss these concerns more deeply?"

That would have been the shift. Five minutes, maybe less. But in those few minutes, the air in the room would have lightened, not tightened. The silence would have broken. And the team would have walked out aligned, knowing the real issues had been named instead of ignored. And, they would have had clarity on the path forward.

That's the power of the Compass Check-In. It isn't complicated. It doesn't take hours. It's about noticing when the room has shifted and being willing to sit in it long enough for the truth to surface. That's how you build momentum that lasts, one truth, one breath, one realignment at a time.

Mirror Moment

When was the last time you paused in a meeting, not for silence, but for clarity, and what shifted because of it?

If I had slowed down in that meeting, here's what I believe would have surfaced, and how it connects back to the Compass.

- **Shira:** "If we aren't clear about readiness, managers will handle these conversations differently, and people will hear mixed messages. That hurts credibility."
  Compass Connection: Values (North). What she was naming was alignment to fairness and honesty, and the risk to credibility when those values get blurred.

- **June:** "When someone believes they're in line for a role they'll never actually get; it can break trust in ways that are hard to repair."
  Compass Connection: Emotions (West). She was pointing to

the emotional fallout, disappointment, betrayal, disconnection, and how it spreads beyond the individual to the culture of the team.

- **Travis:** "Half the names on these lists aren't realistic successors. Until we start saying that out loud, we're not solving the problem."
  Compass Connection: Beliefs (East). He was cutting straight to the stories we tell ourselves, that our bench is strong enough, that putting names in boxes means progress. His push was to replace wishful thinking with truth-telling.
- **Michelle:** "If we want alignment, we can't avoid these conversations. We have to agree on how we'll say the hard thing, not just how we'll run the session."
  Compass Connection: Thoughts (South). Her steadiness was about clarity of approach, about choosing intentional language and a shared framework for action instead of hiding behind process.

That's the power of the Compass Check-In. It shows that what looks like a single point of disagreement is rarely about one thing. Underneath are values, beliefs, thoughts, and emotions, all pressing against each other in real time. When you pause long enough to surface them, you don't lose momentum. You build it, one truth, one breath, one realignment at a time.

I cannot redo that meeting, but I did learn from it. I learned that silence is often a signal, not a success. I learned that staying on track is never the win if it costs you the room. And I learned that trust grows when you pause long enough to name what is real. In the next chapter, we'll take this one step further. Because presence in the moment is powerful, but it is consistency over time that cements trust and makes alignment part of your culture.

Chapter 11

You Go First

I was working with a former colleague, a strong HR leader, who had just taken a major role at a new company. They recruited him for his experience because they knew it was exactly what they needed: a steady hand to guide a culture that had outgrown its old ways. The organization was at a critical point; everyone knew it. The structures that had once worked were now getting in their way. They needed sharper alignment, stronger leadership behaviors, and a shift from comfortable habits to intentional growth. That's why they hired him. Not to maintain what was familiar, but to help lead the change they knew was overdue.

He saw it clearly. He knew what good looked like because he had built it before. The path forward wasn't theoretical; it was practical, proven, and frankly, overdue. But the deeper he moved into the work, the more resistance he encountered. At first, the resistance didn't look like resistance. It looked like polite agreement. Heads nodded in meetings. Action items got written down. No one said no. But behind the nods came slow delays, half-hearted follow-through, and excuses disguised as priorities. *We're waiting on Finance to weigh in. We can't roll this out until Operations is ready. Let's circle back after the next product launch.* By the end of the quarter, the action items were still sitting in the same folder they had been written in.

When he pressed harder, the tone shifted. People started showing up late to meetings, or not at all. Senior leaders would "forget" to include him in side conversations. In strategy sessions, they applauded the concepts in principle but quietly pushed responsibility somewhere else. He called it the *"yes, but not me"* dance. Yes, we should build more accountability. Yes, we should clarify decision rights. Yes, we should shift how we lead. But not here. Not now. Not me. When the spotlight shifted from concept to personal accountability, the appetite for change suddenly had dietary restrictions.

When we sat down to talk about it, his frustration was clear. He said, "They knew who they were hiring. They said they wanted this. Why does it feel like I'm fighting them every step of the way?"

It's a question more leaders should ask out loud. Because the truth is, wanting change for the organization is different from wanting change for yourself. As long as the shift was happening somewhere else, the idea of transformation felt exciting. But when the mirror turned inward, when the expectations reached their own habits, urgency quickly became defensiveness. It wasn't that they didn't want the organization to evolve. They just didn't want to be the ones who had to go first.

I reminded him of something I had learned the hard way: changing a culture is less like turning a jet ski and more like turning a cruise ship. It doesn't pivot on command. It doesn't show signs of progress overnight. But it does move. And when it moves, it leaves a wake, a shift in momentum that, once set into motion, changes the landscape behind it. It requires patience, persistence, and a steady belief that the work, even when invisible, is working.

But metaphors only go so far when you're in the middle of it. So, I offered him something more practical. I sent him the early manuscript of the Evolutionary Mindset model, still unpublished at the time, and asked him to sit with it over the weekend. No agenda. No pressure. Just an invitation to reflect before our next conversation.

When we met for a virtual coffee on Monday morning, something had shifted. His frustration was still there, this work is never without frustration, but underneath it, there was clarity. He said, "I realized I was trying to push them through change, but I hadn't helped them see how to evolve. I was fighting their resistance instead of building their capacity." That realization changes everything.

Because culture work, real culture work, isn't about speed or compliance. It's about evolution. It's not about getting everyone to move faster. It's about helping them move differently. And that starts with leadership that can hold the weight of the work without rushing to resolve it.

It's easy to forget, especially under pressure, that culture is always a mirror, and the reflection is leadership. If a team hesitates, it reflects leadership's hesitation to create space for uncertainty. If a team resists, it reflects leadership's resistance to meet discomfort without blame. If a team disengages, it reflects leadership's failure to connect the work to meaning. What you model, day after day, conversation after conversation, becomes the culture your teams mirror back to you. It doesn't happen through declarations. It happens through demonstration.

The truth is, most change efforts don't fail because of poor strategy. They fail because no one stuck with it long enough for people to believe it mattered. Culture doesn't shift when you roll out something new. It shifts when people start to expect it, when the message matches the meeting, when the energy on launch day still shows up two Tuesdays later, in the middle of a messy calendar and a tired team. That's when people start to trust it. Not because it was perfect, but because it was still there.

Evolution doesn't ask for flash. It asks for rhythm. Anchors create that rhythm. And anchors aren't systems; they're signals. They're the small, intentional practices that tether you back to steadiness when the current pulls you sideways. Think about a leader who pauses before reacting in a tense meeting and simply says, "Let me think about that for a moment." That single pause is an anchor. Or a manager who ends a meeting by asking, "What belief might have been in the room today?" That one question, repeated over time, becomes an anchor. These aren't dramatic gestures. They're small, reliable signals that tell people, *this is how we lead here.* You already have some of these anchors in your hands: the pause of the Intention Gap, that space between impulse and action where your wiring meets your wisdom; the Behavior Compass, which helps you decode what's really driving a reaction; and the Compass Check-In, a minute-long reflection that brings clarity to the heat of a conversation. None of these are complicated. But repeated, they become culture-shaping. Like brushing your teeth, you don't do them because the day is calm, you do them because the day isn't.

I'll be honest: I haven't always modeled this well. I can think of more than one time when the frustration I saw in my team was just a reflection of my own impatience. They weren't dragging their feet; I was rushing them. They weren't confused; I hadn't slowed down enough to clarify. And I can think of another moment when someone finally spoke up in a meeting after weeks of silence, and instead of listening, I rushed to defend the decision. The look on their face told me everything: I had just reinforced why speaking up felt risky. But there have also been moments when I got it right. When I caught myself mid-sentence, realized my tone was sharp, and said, "Let me start over, I came in hot, and that wasn't fair." The room softened instantly. Or the time I ended a difficult meeting by admitting, "I don't have this all figured out yet, but I want to hear what I might be missing." That single statement opened the door for voices that had been quiet all afternoon. Those moments weren't perfect, but they were steady. And the steadiness mattered.

That's the real invitation of the Evolutionary Mindset. Not to be flawless. Not to have it all figured out. But to go first. To reflect the culture, you want to see long before anyone else has proof it will work. And yes, sometimes it will feel like no one notices. You'll pause instead of reacting, or name the emotion in the room, and wonder if it mattered. But culture doesn't move on applause. It moves on pattern. And what you repeat, especially when it would be easier not to, is what your team begins to believe.

Every team reflects something back to its leadership. You may not always like what you see, but that doesn't make it any less yours. If people are guarded, it may be because openness hasn't felt safe. If they're hesitant, it may be because last time someone spoke up, it wasn't received with curiosity. If they're waiting for someone else to go first, that's a signal: leadership hasn't modeled it yet.

And that's where you come in. Because the way your culture sees change will always come back to how you carry it. The wake you leave, steady, intentional, aligned, starts with one simple choice: you go first.

Mirror Moment

If your team is a mirror, what is your leadership reflecting right now and is it aligned with the culture you say you want to build?

I'm not going to pretend that reading this book means your team is now magically immune to change fatigue, or that your nervous system won't still tighten when *business update* lands in your inbox. (Spoiler: mine does too.) But here's what I hope you do leave with: a way to see change differently. A way to name what's actually happening underneath the surface. And a way to lead through it with a little more clarity, steadiness, and maybe even courage.

Now it's your turn to put this into practice. And you don't have to start from scratch. You've got anchors already waiting: the full Evolutionary Mindset Assessment to hold up a mirror, the Behavior Compass to decode what's driving reactions, the Compass Check-In to pause when a conversation goes sideways, the Intention Gap to catch yourself before instinct takes the wheel. They're not big, flashy systems. They're small, repeatable signals that tell your team, *we're still evolving, even in the chaos.*

And if you want to go deeper, you can. There's a community of leaders walking this same road. There are tools and practices you can download, adapt, and share. There's even the chance to become a certified practitioner and bring this framework into your own organization. But you don't have to wait for any of that. You don't need a budget line, a title, or a strategy launch to begin.

Because here's the thing: you don't need to change everything. You just need to change how you carry it.

Evolution doesn't start in the strategy deck. It starts with the one brave person who chooses to lead differently, on purpose.

Let it be you.

After all maybe you were made for such a time as this.

References

Fitzduff, M. (2021). *The Amygdala Hijack*. In *Our Brains at War: The Neuroscience of Conflict and Peacebuilding* (pp. 25–35). Oxford Academic.

Korn Ferry. (2023). *A guide to mastering organizational culture change*. Retrieved from https://www.kornferry.com

McKinsey & Company. (2023, April 26). *The State of Organizations 2023: Ten shifts transforming organizations*. Retrieved from McKinsey & Company.

Rabinoff, M., et al. (2015). *Fear and the defense cascade: Clinical implications and neurobiological mechanisms*. Frontiers in Behavioral Neuroscience, 9, Article 292. Retrieved from PM.

Hebb, D. O. (1949). *The Organization of Behavior: A Neuropsychological Theory*. Wiley.

Chomse, M., Roos, L., Misra, R., & Whillans, A. (2025, June 4). *Employee stress is a business risk, not an HR problem*. Harvard Business Review. Retrieved from Harvard Business Review.

Kahneman, D., & Tversky, A. (1974). *Judgment under uncertainty: Heuristics and biases*. Science, 185(4157), 1124–1131.

Colier, N. (2018, December 5). *Fear: False evidence appearing real?* Psychology Today. https://www.psychologytoday.com/us/blog/inviting-monkey-tea/201812/fear-false-evidence-appearing-real

Samuelson, W., & Zeckhauser, R. (1988). Status quo bias in decision making. *Journal of Risk and Uncertainty*, 1(1), 7–59.

Kahneman, D., & Tversky, A. (1979). Prospect theory: An analysis of decision under risk. *Econometrica*, 47(2), 263–291.

Grant, A. (2021). Think again: The power of knowing what you don't know. Viking.

Edmondson, A. C. (2019). *The fearless organization: Creating psychological safety in the workplace for learning, innovation, and growth.* Wiley.

Jost, J. T., Banaji, M. R., & Nosek, B. A. (2004). A decade of system justification theory: Accumulated evidence of conscious and unconscious bolstering of the status quo. *Political Psychology, 25*(6), 881–919.

Acknowledgments

First and foremost, I give thanks to God, who has guided every step of this journey. This book is not just a reflection of my work, but a testimony of His faithfulness in giving me the courage, wisdom, and endurance to keep moving forward.

To my family, your love and encouragement reminded me daily of what matters most. You gave me space when I needed to write, strength when I felt weary, and joy when I needed perspective.

To my mentors, colleagues, and friends, thank you for speaking truth into my life, challenging me to grow, and reminding me that leadership is never a solo endeavor.

To the leaders, HR professionals, and teams I've had the privilege of walking alongside, you've taught me more than you know. Your willingness to wrestle with change and choose courage over comfort has shaped this message in ways theory never could.

Finally, to every reader, may this book point you toward a mindset that doesn't just manage change, but embraces evolution with clarity, steadiness, and hope. My prayer is that you find encouragement in these pages and the courage to lead with purpose and intention.

With gratitude,
Amy

About the Author

Amy Washburn is a leadership strategist, culture builder, and trusted advisor to organizations navigating today's fast-changing world of work. With more than 20 years of experience as an HR executive, Amy has led cultural transformations, coached senior leadership teams, and built high-performance environments where innovation, resilience, and human connection drive success. Through her company, Shift HR Consulting, she equips leadership teams and HR professionals with practical tools to help organizations not just manage change but evolve through it. Amy's work is grounded in strategic insight, a deep understanding of human dynamics, and an unwavering belief that leadership starts with presence, humility, and courage. When she's not writing, speaking, or coaching, you can usually find her centering herself on a hiking trail with her family or grounding her mornings in prayer, practices that fuel both her faith and her leadership. She believes the quiet moments are where clarity, resilience, and purpose are forged

Before You Go...

I'm not going to pretend that reading this book means your team is now magically immune to change fatigue or that your nervous system won't still tighten when "business update" lands in your inbox. (Spoiler: mine does too.)

But here's what I hope you *do* leave with:

A way to *see* change differently. A way to *name* what's actually happening underneath the surface. And a way to *lead* through it with a little more clarity, steadiness, and maybe even a little courage. Now it's your turn to put this into practice. And you don't have to start from scratch.

Want to go deeper? You've got options.

- **Take the full Evolutionary Mindset Assessment**
  Download the 50-question self-assessment, tally your own score, and use the results worksheet to break down what your answers reveal. You'll see where you're strong, where you may be stuck, and how to take your next step forward.

- **Grab the Behavior Compass tools**
  Print them. Hang them where you can see them. Use them before that tense meeting you're already dreading.

- **Use the Compass Check-In with your team**
  You don't need a big speech. Just pause. Ask what feels off. And be willing to name what's real.

- **Download the reflection worksheets**

    These are bite-sized, no-fluff tools designed for actual humans, not robots pretending they have it all figured out.

You can find all of these at:

TheEvolutionaryMindset.com/Tools

If you're looking for support beyond the page, I'm available for consulting and speaking engagements to help you bring the Evolutionary Mindset to life inside your organization. Because here's the thing, you don't need to change everything. You just need to change how you *carry* it. Evolution doesn't start in the strategy deck. It starts with the one brave person who chooses to lead differently, on purpose.

Let it be you.

Worksheets & Tools

The Evolutionary Mindset

By Amy Washburn

The Behavior Compass Worksheet

Use the questions below and the graphics on the following page to identify your Values, Beliefs, Thoughts, and Emotions related to a current change you are navigating.

Current Change:
_____
_____

Values: Are my core values helping or hindering my ability to navigate change?

Beliefs: Are my beliefs supporting an Evolutionary Mindset, or am I stuck in outdated perspectives?

Thoughts: How is my thinking affecting my ability to adapt?

Emotions: How are my emotions shaping my change experience?

_____
_____
_____

Advantages of Current Behavior What is working well?	**Disadvantages of Current Behavior** What is holding me back?
Advantages of Current Behavior What could be beneficial to explore?	**Disadvantages of Current Behavior** What challenges might come from shifting my approach?

Current

New

Copyright 2025

Visual Graphics

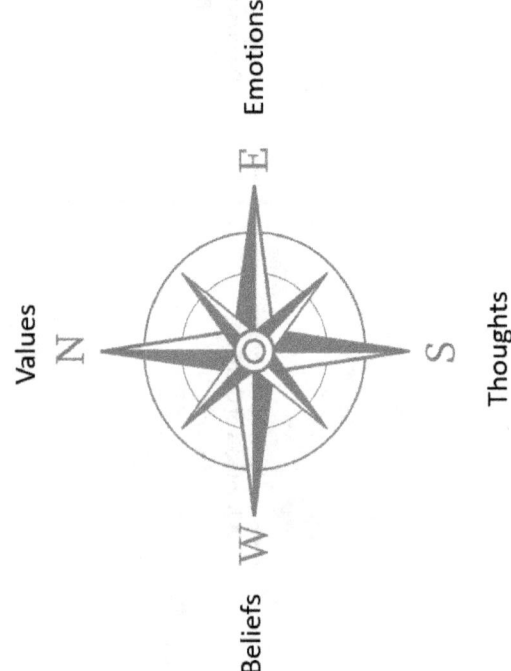

The Evolutionary Mindset

	N	E	S	W
	Values	Beliefs	Thoughts	Emotions
B				
E	Provides Stability	Evolutionary Mindset	Strategic Thinking	Drives Engagement
H	Guides Decision-Making	Fosters Innovation	Solution Focused	Fosters Connection
A	Creates Resilience	Enhances Adaptability	Communicate with Clarity	Enhances Motivation
V				
—	—	—	—	—
I	Rigid Thinking	Uncertainty Paralysis	Avoid Difficult Decisions	Clouded Judgement
O	Resistant to new ideas	Identity Crisis	Struggle with Conflict	Fear-Based Resistance
R	Moral High Ground	Group Influence	Deprioritizes Results	Inconsistency

Strength (above dividing line) · Weakness (below dividing line)

Copyright 2025

The Evolutionary Mindset

By Amy Washburn

The Behavior Mapping Worksheet

The Behavior Compass shows us that values, beliefs, thoughts, and emotions drive what we do. This worksheet helps you map those drivers, your own or someone else's, so you can see what's really underneath and shift with clarity.

Simply work through each Compass point, writing down what's activated, and then reflect on what alignment would look like instead.

Step 1: Identify the Behavior

What behavior is showing up? (e.g., avoidance, defensiveness, shutdown, over-controlling, etc.)

Behavior:

_____

Step 2: Map the Current State

Use the compass directions below to reflect on what may be driving the behavior.

North – VALUES: What value feels activated or threatened right now?

Response:

_____

_____

East – BELIEFS: What belief might be driving this behavior? Is it still true or just familiar?

Response:

_____

_____

_____

South – THOUGHTS: What internal script or story is playing on repeat?

Response:

_____

_____

_____

West – EMOTIONS: What emotion is present underneath the surface?

Response:

_____

_____

_____

Step 3: Map the Desired State

What would alignment look like across the compass points?

North – VALUES:

_____

East – BELIEFS:

_____

South – THOUGHTS:

_____

West – EMOTIONS:

_____

Step 4: Reflect on the Gap

What's holding you back from shifting? Where can you practice a new approach in a low-stakes moment?

Notes:

_____

_____

_____

_____

_____

The Evolutionary Mindset

By Amy Washburn

The Intention Gap Quick Guide

Use these six micro-practices in the moment, when the meeting is tense, your jaw is tight, and your instinct is to react. Print it. Tape it to your laptop. Use it when it counts.

1. Name the Signal

Notice when you're activated: tight jaw, racing thoughts, urge to interrupt. Say it: "I/m activated. This matters." Naming it is the cue to pause.

2. Buy a Beat

Literally—pause. Take one breath. Sip your water. Say something like, "Let me think about that for a second," or "I want to make sure I'm answering this clearly." Give logic time to catch up with emotion.

3. Check the Compass

Ask: What value just got hit? What belief flared up? What thought is spinning? What emotion is tugging at you? You don't have to fix it in the moment—just naming it breaks the autopilot.

4. Reset Your Body

Your nervous system listens to your posture more than your thoughts. Drop your shoulders. Unclench your jaw. Plant your feet. Sit back or stand tall. Signal to your system: "I'm safe. I'm steady. I'm still leading."

5. Use an Anchor Phrase

Keep a sticky note on your laptop, your planner, or wherever you tend to get activated. It could say: "Respond, don't react." Or "Pause to lead." Or even "Hold space, not control." Words only work if they're repeated. Make it a habit, not a gimmick.

6. Call in a Signal Buddy

Sometimes you're too in it to notice. That's when you need someone in the room who can give you the "nose swipe" or send the "Slow down" message in chat. Agree on the signal ahead of time. Tell them what your signals are. Let them help you catch yourself before the reactivity wins.

The Evolutionary Mindset

By Amy Washburn

Trigger Reflection Worksheet

Use this worksheet to reflect on a specific moment when you felt emotionally triggered. This tool is designed to help you uncover the story behind your reaction and trace it through your Behavior Compass: Values (North), Beliefs (East), Thoughts (South), and Emotions (West).

Step 1: Describe the Triggering Moment
What happened? Be specific.

_____

_____

_____

Step 2: What Did You Feel?
List the emotion(s) you experienced in that moment.

_____

_____

_____

Step 3: What Story Did You Tell Yourself?
What internal narrative or assumption showed up? Examples: 'They don't value me,' 'I'm going to fail,' 'This always happens to me.'

_____

_____

_____

_____

Step 4: Trace the Compass

Use the Behavior Compass to identify what got activated.

North – VALUES: What value of yours may have been challenged?

_____

East – BELIEFS: What belief did this moment reinforce or threaten?

_____

South – THOUGHTS: What thought started looping in your mind?

_____

West – EMOTIONS: What emotion drove your response?

_____

Step 5: Reframe the Story

What's another story you could tell yourself about this moment?

_____

_____

Step 6: Moving Forward with Intention

What could you do differently next time a similar trigger shows up?

The Evolutionary Mindset

By Amy Washburn

Compass Check-In

The Compass Check-In isn't about analyzing or fixing. It's about noticing what's real, naming it, and choosing the next intentional move. You can run it in your head, walk the team through it out loud, or jot it on a sticky note. It doesn't need to be polished. It just needs to be real.

But remember this only works if you've done your own work first. If you haven't explored your own Compass, your values, beliefs, inner narratives, and emotional triggers, this will land flat. Alignment starts with you. When tension rises, energy dips, or silence gets heavy, use R.E.A.L.:

R: Read the Room

Individual: What feels off in me right now?

Team: What just shifted in the room: tone, energy, silence, disengagement? Name it out loud so no one has to pretend it didn't happen.

E: Explore What's Being Protected

Individual: What might I be guarding—status, identity, control, or belonging?

Team: What might the group be protecting beneath the surface? Curiosity disarms defensiveness. Look underneath, not at who's "causing the problem."

A: Activate the Compass

Individual: What might I be guarding—status, identity, control, or belonging?

Team: What might the group be protecting beneath the surface?

L: Lead the Shift

Individual: What's one intentional move I can make right now (pause, reframe, invite, acknowledge)?

Team: What's one intentional move we can make together?

www.ingramcontent.com/pod-product-compliance
Lightning Source LLC
Chambersburg PA
CBHW050557170426
43201CB00011B/1726